PATRICIA PALMORE

CHOOSING TO CHANGE

Changing My Will
Changed My Life

ISBN: 978-1-09836-631-5 (print)
ISBN: 978-1-09836-632-2 (eBook)

TABLE OF CONTENTS

ACKNOWLEDGEMENTS

To my biological and spiritual families and every mentor God assigned to guide me, thank you. To each friend, advisor, editor, coach, encourager, and those who prayed without ceasing for me to complete this project, thank you.

To my paternal grandmother, Lucille Johnson Turner: Thank you for more than seventy years of prayers for God's plan to unfold. Your devotion to God captured our attention and our hearts. Watching you worship Jesus and study His Word changed our lives.

DEDICATIONS

To my first-born, the son of my strength: Glenn P. Brooks, Jr. You inspired me when you said, "Ma, did it ever occur to you somebody's life will stay stuck, if you don't finish writing your book?"

To my precious daughter, Candice: Your laughter and positivity encouraged me to believe I could laugh through mistakes and keep going for the finish!

To my mother, Essie: You *always* believed in me and caused me to believe in myself whenever you said, "Oh, I *know* you can!"

INTRODUCTION

One day, driving toward a traffic light at a busy intersection, my attention had been on my destination, music on the radio, other drivers and pedestrians. The last thing I expected to see was a little grey squirrel there, looking frightened and confused. Poised to act, he frantically, glanced in one direction and then the next.

Instantly, as though someone had shoved a zoomed image of his tiny face before my eyes, *I felt* his fear and confusion intensify as he contemplated what to do. Somehow, I could sense the gravity of his situation; he was feeling pressed and "out on a limb". I wondered what he would do. Would he try to scamper across the busy intersection in a flash or would he reverse his direction? In that moment, he seemed paralyzed with indecision and my heart almost broke watching his apparent helplessness.

Instantly, I heard God's Spirit profoundly whisper, "This is how my children feel when, because of their foolish and ignorant choices, they find themselves suddenly halted, debilitated by crisis, and fearing life-threatening dilemmas." Within the calm and safety of His voice, I sensed His infinite compassion for us; I actually "felt" His love and willingness to help us, *if only* we would call *to Him* for help!

Our Creator and heavenly Father chose to make our human bodies from earthly elements. He also knows we are immature—limited in our focus and composure. Often, we stray from our charted paths during fear or confusion, not knowing which way to turn.

If God saw the little squirrel's dilemma, how much more has He seen yours and mine? Don't you think He knows when you and I feel trapped, when our thoughts are spinning off course? Yet, He considers us His master creation and crowning achievement! He knows every decision we contemplate and each direction we should take because He created us. He assigned us to tend the earth and rule over the business of earthly affairs, delegating to us authority to enforce His righteous standard over the rest of His creation. Our Master-mission is to maintain an atmosphere of godliness on earth, as it is in heaven.

Through many mistakes in judgment, I discovered godly solutions to my problems were always available, *if* I had asked God to reveal them. A rich store of godly wisdom for handling every choice I faced was available too, *if* I had chosen to dust off (and read) His instruction manual.

We all can choose to swallow our pride and consult the Bible for answers or we can try to figure out life by ourselves. The more we read God's instruction manual, the better our decisions can be. God created each of us as unique. He wants us to slow down, listen and follow His specific instructions. Regardless of the situation, He can help us make right calls because He knows exactly what each of us needs. Nothing surprises Him—He knows everything. Even before a situation occurs, He knows. He knows the reason (and season) for which He commissioned each of us to live in the earth, and He can tell each of us the end of a matter before it begins. Before He created Earth or filled it with life of every kind, He already knew we would need His help to live here successfully as He intended. He knows it's all a "matter of our will".

People and events can influence our choices, but no one can make us choose against our will. We must weigh options and consequences, before deciding to take action. Then we deal with the consequences of our actions.

God gives us freedom (and permission) to approach Him in prayer, and simply ask Him to help us choose the right action or course.

He can make all things work together for our good in spite of wrong choices.

CHAPTER ONE

Changing Amid Childhood Influences

Influences of Ethnicity and Diversity

Growing up, my mother sometimes chuckled as she said, "Patricia, it seems like you have to eat the whole cow before you know you've had beef." I now admit she was right. However, once I finally "got it" (whatever the "it" was that I needed to understand), I was usually good to go! Eventually, her meaning became clearer as I grew and matured. Meanwhile, God's Holy Spirit would whisper wisdom I needed to know or nudge me to trust Him, in spite of my lack of understanding. I began to regard these moments as "my God moments".

Born at home, my mother said I was slow even to breathe. Interestingly, she also said I was born with something she, her mother, and the midwife referred to as a "veil" covering my face. They seemed to think it meant my birth was different for some reason—a reason I never really understood, unless God showed me.

Mama told me she had been sickly as a young woman, severely anemic while pregnant with my three older siblings. She said she usually weighed just under 100 pounds. In contrast, she said with me she felt fine the entire nine months and her appetite was better than ever! She said I was the largest of the five of us, weighing in at 8 pounds. Hearing these facts always made me feel special. I grew up a quiet child, as compared to a few of my siblings, and longed to resemble Mama because my brother and three sisters looked more like her. (For me, "normal" meant being like everyone else). Years later, Mama surprised me as she laughingly told me how my father had wanted at least one of us to look more like him. Then she confided why (she believed) I looked different.

You see, Mama's mother was half Native American and half Irish American, so most relatives on her side of the family were tall with a lighter skin tone. (Maybe this accounted for my middle sister's blue eyes and light skin tone at birth. In fact, all my siblings' skin was lighter.

Since Daddy knew Mama's father was of African descent, as were his own parents, both he and Mama were a little surprised, prior to my birth, genetics had not selected a darker skin gene from the gene pool. (My younger sister would also have lighter skin when she was born two years later, a fact he couldn't have known.) So I think Daddy might have been hoping God would grant his heart's desire for a color match with at least one of his babies). Mama said he found many ways to "hint" at this desire, without openly saying what was on his mind. So, she kept praying and asking God (though she confesses she didn't know much about praying back then), "Dear God, please make this baby as black as coal, so he can be satisfied."

When I arrived in the world on that chilly morning of January 23rd, my mother said I looked like "a spitting image" of my Dad! The only major difference was I was female! Mama remembers laughing at his reaction to me when he first saw me. She said, "His face said it all; his smile was so wide, a jack-o-lantern paled in comparison!"

Later, she laughingly revealed her secret thought, though she didn't dare voice it at the time. She said she just smiled inwardly, thinking, "I hope this one is dark enough for you!" Among all his children, I was the only one of us who shared Daddy's darker complexion, body type and full lips. We looked more like the Johnsons (his side of our family). I know he loved all his children, though I think my birth might have been a time when God actually "winked" at him.

Throughout my life, I wrestled with changing my "acquired mindset" about the real and the perceived differences a person's skin tone, (or eye color, or height or other physical traits), contributes to the quality of their relationships with people.

To this day, I think our adversary, Satan, has managed to deceive us by perverting the importance of something as harmless as skin color, or ethnicity, or nationality or body type to a level of jealousy and bitter hostility. Instead of accepting our physical traits, purely, as God's creative love for expressing aesthetic beauty through diverse colors, sizes, shapes, and gifts, (as He did with the rest of His creation), we have contaminated it. Many ignore God's own statement of approval when sealing his crowning achievement on the day He finished creating humanity, calling us "very good".

In my teen years, my Daddy (who was a gifted artist in portraits and caricature) explained racial prejudice to me. He sat me down, looked at me intently, and said gently, "Baby, never hate other people for any reason, especially because of the color of their skin. They didn't choose what color they would be. Besides if you return the hate you receive from others, it makes you guilty of their offense. Hate is still hate, no matter who's doing the hating, and hate destroys, *period*." In short, he was telling me people are just people. So, don't be too quick to believe what others say about someone. First, get to know him or her, and slowly form your own opinion with wisdom, patience and understanding. His explanation was so simple and true; I decided that day, "I will change 'how' I hear the racial concerns and undertones of others."

To this day, I agree with my Dad—not simply because he was my Dad—but because his assessment of the so-called racial situation agrees with the Biblical account of God's truth. So far, his perspective on this subject has proved to be "spot on". Everything God created, He called "good and very good". I've chosen to believe this as I mine the precious ore buried deep inside people I engage. Mining can be dark and dangerous, but finding precious treasure in each of them makes my effort worthwhile.

Traumatized by Tragedy

In elementary school, I found myself feeling fearful as I heard about real-life accounts of human-on-human violence. I looked for relief from the shocking images branded in my mind. Though I was too young to "define peace", I knew I needed some way to escape fear.

At ten years old, I actually heard a profound inner voice threaten me, "You'll never make it to eleven years old." It made my heart race! Then one day after school, my oldest sister recounted how a classmate's brother-in-law had tragically stabbed her classmate to death while she babysat for them. The grisly details of the murder made my flesh crawl. I never dreamed a family member could do such a thing to their loved one! Each time I overheard the gruesome details, I began to live in silent fear.

Finally, while my parents were at work, I picked up their Bible and started reading it. (Daddy and Mama tried to reassure us during hard-hitting tragedies like this, but fear still gripped me at unexpected moments). Rather than talk about how I felt, I tried to mask my fears by acting carefree like other children around me. Feeling vulnerable, I preferred being indoors, unless I was at school or church.

Soon, I started reading and immersing my mind in fairy tales, because they made me feel safe while the story lasted, and fantasies always had happy-endings! Still hungering for soul peace and safety, a powerful thought came to mind: I had been recalling some of my parents' conversations about God. They were always excited when they talked about how God rescued them from scary situations. From time to time, they even retold those stories, saying how they had learned to trust God's strength to take them through all kinds of things! I embraced that glimmer of hope and began reading my parents' Bible while they were at work, as best I could understand it. I can't explain what drove me to read their Bible, except a strong and distinct thought urged me, "Read the Bible". Soon afterward, my parents noticed, and a few months later, they gave me my very first book of Children's Bible Stories and my own Little Golden Book of religious Christmas carols, as a bonus!

I was ecstatic as the *real* stories of David and Goliath, the three Hebrew boys and others, quickly started erasing my fears; I finally felt some peace. I gained more courage and confidence as I read about their bravery! I didn't know it at the time, but reading my Children's Bible was redirecting my focus *from* tragedy to calm. Each time I read about Noah's Ark or Adam and Eve, a settled peace made me feel safe. (I do recall being upset at Eve, though, because I thought she had messed up everything for everybody! I didn't know God was working details of His plan together, even then, for everyone's good).

When I learned Jesus is God's Son, I loved Him right away! As I began shifting my focus away from my inabilities and insecurities to the strength and power of God, I felt safer and happier! Reading my little Bible, I learned how this good God had sent Jesus to earth in a human body to restore relationship between Himself and people. It reassured me! Now, reading my Bible out of interest—not fear, God even delivered me from fear of thunderstorms and bullies! I discovered Jesus is very much alive and active in our lives, whether or not we realize it. He still directs me, repositions people and rearranges situations to work together for my good, and for the good of them who love to obey Him.

Understanding My Human Design

As a three-part (triune) being, I must remember my body is "my earth suit", connecting me with the earthly, the tangible and the measurable. My soul (housing my mind, heart, emotions and will) is conscious of God and connects me to both spirit *and* earth realms.

My human spirit (the essential and eternal me) connects me to God's realm, making me God-conscious as I read His written Word. Our spiritual adversary wages battle in the "middle ground" (the mind), where we must strive to choose God's truth over our preferences of convenience and self-gratification.

Looking back, I realize God always had a good plan for me (see Jeremiah 29:11). The thief (the devil) had a plan for my life, too; he wanted to steal from me, kill me, destroy me and devour me! As if that were not enough, my body of flesh also has a plan to get what it needs to meet my physical needs. These legitimate fleshy appetites can quickly form unhealthy habits, if I indulge them too regularly or if I exceed my body's requirements for them. They use the channels of my normal sense of sight, smell, taste, hearing, and touch because I need those five senses to help my body function. Listen to God's wise voice of caution:

"Just because something is technically legal doesn't mean that it's spiritually appropriate. If I went around doing whatever I thought I could get by with, I'd be a slave to my whims."

(I Corinthians 6:12 MSG)

God breathed my human spirit (the real me) into this body of flesh, therefore I am "like God" because I'm made in His image (spirit). I learned that to be spiritually strong, my spirit must, first, desire the spiritual things God wants me to know. So I strengthen those desires by feeding my spirit with "spiritual" food: Reading and meditating God's Word, praying regularly and spending intimate time talking with Him, and worshipping in His presence. Diligently practicing these habits began erasing some of my destructive cravings until they warred less against my human spirit. I started getting a little better at judging how to handle what I perceived through my five senses. (Only a wise human spirit can determine healthy boundaries for satisfying bodily needs). God's Word helps prevent my immature will and unbridled emotions from joining forces against my mind.

The power and wisdom in God's Word also helps me guard my eyes, ears, nose, mouth, and touch. (As habits developed from my pattern of choices, my will and my flesh started preferring those habits, so when stronger desires overruled right choices, my health and wellness suffered). Wise choices, on the other hand, can derail satanic schemes that aim to sabotage my health and relationships, so I learned to guard my strong desires and seek more wisdom.

*The Bible places "strong desires" into three categories: The lust of the flesh, the lust of the eyes, and the pride of life. My flesh nature operates within the realm for which God designed it to function: the physical realm, so it will satisfy natural cravings, without regard for God's desires, God's plan, or God's timetable. Unless restrained, my flesh will get what it wants, as much as it wants, whenever it wants, and however it wants, as long as it "feels" good. As an untaught child, my flesh is ignorant of the plan God has for my life, so I learned to short circuit its yearnings.

When I finally read Jeremiah 29:10-14, I discovered God had planned good things for me, but too often, I didn't want to wait for Him to lead me to them. Many times, I failed the test of maturity when handling some details of God's plan as I received them. Sometimes I rushed in, puffed up, thinking I knew what was best for all concerned. Often, I based my decisions on whether things *appeared* good or safe at the time. That's how I found out immature behavior is often headstrong and prideful; too often, that described me. Early on, I learned God doesn't need to battle with humans, nor does He arm-wrestle with us; it would be an unfair fight. You see, He is Sovereign. He has already told us His Word is *always* right (Psalms 33:4-9), and His counsel *shall* stand (Psalms 160:119).

Some truths I learned from following and encountering God: (1) When my will conflicts with God's will, He simply waits. He waits for me to discover my way will never succeed, until I submit my will to His. In fact, doing things "my way" was a sure recipe for disaster. Doing things "my way" resulted in me crawling back into God's presence for forgiveness, and I'm glad He was always there waiting with abundant mercy! (2) Sometimes, God has urged me, "Do it now". At other times, He simply instructed me to "wait". Maybe He wanted me to wait because I tended to want the exact opposite of what He knew was best for me.

This was true, especially in my younger years, when my natural appetites were stronger than my newly reborn spirit. After a while, I noticed the more I messed up, the harder I struggled to get up. This process of getting back up actually proved constructive in the long run, because it caused the "struggling me" to give up and go back to God for forgiveness and advice. As I learned to change my mind and do what His Word prescribed, I found renewed wisdom to avoid repeating previous mistakes in judgment. Eventually, I began to walk more steadily in God and mess up a little less. In spite of mishaps, the solid reinforcement of God's truth began establishing my decisions.

"For if there is, first, a willing mind, it is accepted according to what one has and not according to what he does not have." (I Corinthians 8:12 NKJV). The Message Translation reads, *"Your heart's been in the right place all along. You've got what it takes to finish it up, so go to it. Once the commitment is clear, do what you can, not what you can't. The heart regulates the hands...."*

Throughout the Bible, God keeps showing me the wisdom (and reward) of a willing heart and mind. He reminds me both regret and loss happen whenever shortsightedness makes me fight against His all-knowing will.

I Samuel, Chapter 25 clearly illustrates the benefits of making right decisions and the consequences of choosing wrong ones. (Set aside some time to read the whole chapter). It's the account of David, the King-in-Waiting and Nabol, a rich fool, who only cared about partying and indulging his bodily appetites instead of protecting his home. His stinginess and indifference provoked David's anger. Too late, he realized his recklessness had provoked a death sentence on his entire household. When he sobered up to this reality, his heart failed, and only God's grace spared Nabol's wife and those in his household.

On this side of the New Testament, I've had many choices to either wait on God's perfect timing or take matters into my own hands. I would love to say I waited for God's plan to unfold, but I didn't always "want" to wait, nor did I even know "how" to wait. Often, I thought I knew more than God and those He appointed to guide me.

A Flashback Moment

When I first learned to ride the bike I shared with my siblings, I asked my middle sister to show me how to ride. (I was never a very athletic kid, and aside from being able to run fast, I spent most of my time with my nose in a book, writing poems, or drawing).

That day as others breezed happily past me, I decided I wanted to enjoy the fun and freedom of it all! As my sister began explaining where I should place my feet and hands, I interrupted her, saying, "Thanks, I got it. I see how to do it!" I was convinced I understood how to ride a bike; it seemed so easy.

Right away, I jumped onto the bike and started riding. It *was* easy. Feeling quite proud of myself, I rode the bike smoothly and confidently down the street, around the corner, and into the alley behind the building where we lived. Then, as I rounded the corner and glanced toward the end of the alley, I panicked! (I had forgotten the alley behind our row of homes was short and dead-ended, and now my heart sank fast at what I saw)! The bicycle was speeding up by this time, and I was heading straight for a loaded boxcar, connected to a train parked at the end of the alley! Frantically, I thought, "How do I make this thing stop?" (My arrogance had me assuming I knew all about the ease of riding a bike. Now I realized I hadn't waited long enough to hear "all" the instructions, like how to stop it)!

By this time, even fear had deserted me, and dread had taken its place. Desperately looking around for a way to stop, the only thing I saw was a large, heavy-metal ash can (prevalent back then in neighborhoods where coal fueled our furnaces). Deliberately (but reluctantly), I headed straight for the can! I hadn't planned to end my wonderful bike ride like I did, but slamming into a parked train was NOT an option I wanted even to consider! My bike hit the big black can (with me on it), knocking it over and spilling ashes all over my clothes, my hair, my face and the bike! Embarrassed and humiliated, I slowly stood up—trying to brush away all of that ash!

Yep, my first bike ride had been memorable, to say the least, but not in the way I had expected. If only I had been more patient and less arrogant, thinking I knew it all! If only I had paid more attention to the details, instead of just the joy of the ride, with the wind swooshing past my face. If only I'd been more respectful and patient, allowing my sister to thoroughly explain the how-to's; and if only I had waited to hear ALL the instructions, I would now be "happily remembering" my first bike ride. As it stands, I will always remember the humiliating lesson of learning patience the hard way, which was (no doubt) the lesson I really needed to learn that day. I am glad I didn't die for my arrogance (as many have done), but I can tell you it's true, pride really does go before destruction, and over confidence really does precede a fall! Today, I greatly respect warning signs, but sadly, I still made other unwise decisions, even humiliating and embarrassing people close to or in authority over me. It took a while before I learned to *not* battle against God's wisdom.

These were accounts of when I was a little slow to "get it" (recalling Mama's observations). They forced me to be still and listen, before executing my self-centered plans. Those awkward lessons taught me the value of seeking wisdom from many trusted and proven counselors, as I wait to be sure God is advising me *before* I move forward with the assurance of His settled peace in my heart.

"A hurried spirit is not of God." –*J. N. Norris*

Wisdom Word: Whoever chooses to wait on God's timing becomes more patient in restraining themselves, through self-discipline, until God is ready to act on their behalf. While waiting feels uncomfortable and inconvenient, finding God's leading and His positive direction always works best, as we become willing to wait.

More Than Flashing Lights

Are you poised to start noticing changes happening around you, which affect your life or business? Remember: Inspiration is just the "beginning" of change. Inspiration is born when God "breathes out" His Word of revealed truth into your spirit, and you receive it with a willing heart. As it ignites, it engages your emotions, propelling you into creative motion. By itself, inspiration (a heavenly substance) is unfruitful, unless it joins with earthly substance to become tangible and measurable.

Feelings, on the other hand, only serve as "flashing lights" to identify a change you must choose (or not) to engage. I'm learning to control my emotions, so

I can redirect my energy toward what "God wants". He never designed emotions to be the long-burning fuel in my furnace, although they can *start* to ignite my move into action. You (and I) must add diligent effort in the right direction to finish making and forming what inspiration reveals. "We" must keep working toward our vision, doing something with it each day, until our efforts produce tangible and accurate "evidence" of a finished work. Inspiration is wonderful to see, feel, touch, read or measure when it fully manifests. However, only when your part (and mine) is complete, will God give us "a sure knowledge" confirming the work is finished. In summary, inspiration is a "divine spark" (the potential and the power) from the Holy Spirit igniting God's desire within the will to DO something on His behalf (not *for* God, but for others, *with* God's help).

Even when I didn't feel inspired, I've learned to pray, "Lord, You are who I seek first, then your guidance comes. I reach for You now with my spirit. Draw me closer so I can touch You and know your heart with my spirit. Amen."

I've learned I hear God better, when I deliberately pull my focus from distractions to embrace an emancipating moment of thanks, adoration, conviction or answered prayer. As I linger in God's presence, the power of the Holy Spirit hovers over my human spirit, waiting for me to say, "Yes" to God's will. His Holy Spirit works in spite of my surroundings. He works all my circumstances together to accomplish exactly what agrees with God's plan for me. All He needs is my cooperation.

Like a potter watching the precious formation of his newest clay vessel, God has always kept His hand on me, shaping, influencing, diligently working together the good, the bad, the painful and the pleasant for my good and His glory! God frequently reminds me, "Pat, don't get stuck in the emotional mire, waiting to 'feel' like it. Look around yourself; be vigilant and seize opportunities. Watching is active, so don't be lazy. Be willing to change quickly and keep changing, whenever and however you must. Lick your wounds if you need to, but keep moving toward your goal and changing until the work is done."

I sense Him now, saying, "Learn from whatever you cannot change, and for now, choose to change your attitude concerning it. Stay on ready and keep on doing and changing whenever and wherever you can, or when changing is the wiser option. Refrain from allowing distractions to hinder, and regrets to linger. Change what you can, as soon as you can, and *wait for Me* to change what you cannot handle."

He exhorts us to make peace, stay at peace and *think* peaceful thoughts! (Even a simpleton knows the last thing a burning building needs is more heat and flame—IF you want to save it!) Doing good can put out flames and pay off for everyone, so keep doing good for good reasons.

Flashback to My Hiding Place

For as far back as I can remember, I wasted too much time and energy trying to get attention "I thought" I deserved—LOVE. Focused on what I wanted, I blocked myself from seeing the truth: God *already* took care of my love deficit, having loved me with His perfect, sacrificial love in just the kind, quality and measure I needed for every situation. He gave me loving parents, who trained (and reared) me in the way I should go. However, as I accepted advice from many so-called friends, I began believing their misinformation. The lie I believed was: I'm not important because others don't notice me. This thinking excused me from engaging in life to stay comfortably inactive. I wonder if this was the reason others sometimes called me "slow" or "lazy"?

In school, my assertiveness had dropped so low until a dark "mood of neglect" brooded in my soul. Laziness and self-pity whispered lies they hoped I would believe. Unfortunately, as I allowed my mind to wallow in self-pity, other negative emotions hitched a ride with them. Soon I began feeling emotionally battered and bruised; I couldn't seem to bounce back!

The more my emotions suffered, more desperation set in. Neglect and indifference can make children feel isolated (even among family).

Confession: I was quiet and timid most of the time. I sought refuge in the one thing I knew would bring sure satisfaction and immediate comfort: FOOD. Food made me feel attractive, confident, and contented, but only temporarily. When I ate for the wrong reasons, the "pleasure" of eating became my preferred "sedative". I later learned eating excessively is what some children do to self-medicate. I didn't know why food was always on my mind. Sometimes I wasn't even hungry, but if someone offered me food, I'd eat because it made me feel happy and accepted. When family members left the table, I'd glance at their plates to check for untouched food. I knew their eating habits, and I figured I could always count on my youngest sister leaving the "nice stuff" on her plate; she was a picky eater. I rarely missed a chance to eat more than my share. Eventually, I learned most children live in the realm of their feelings, as I did, which is part of what categorizes them as immature. They can't always explain what they need or why, but they do *feel* needy and lonely sometimes, as did I. Maybe I was normal after all!

Growing older, I felt like the ugly duckling must have felt because I was shorter, my lips were larger, my body type was a little "thicker" and my skin tone was darker than my family. Whenever playmates teased me about having "big lips", I felt a sting because I couldn't change them. Then I'd try even harder to please or impress them to accept me. Criticism and comparison drove me to be dissatisfied with my appearance, especially during puberty when acne viciously attacked, leaving dark marks and enlarged pores in its wake!

I was reluctant to go to neighborhood dances because I thought no one wanted to dance with a "wallflower", especially one with painful and inflamed acne in plain view!

Even after seeing a dermatologist, he recommended decreasing many of my fried comfort foods, depressing me even more. My middle sister also suffered with acne and was sometimes sad or disappointed with her skin, too and I would feel sad with her. I would feel no peace until she felt okay. I wanted her to hurry and cheer up, so I could feel okay too. How mixed up was that?

Sudden Change

Something unusual happened at school, surprising even me! Though I had convinced myself I was not very intellectual or academic, I happened to score a lot better on a written test than the rest of my classmates; everyone looked surprised, but pleased! I was surprised too. My classmates praised me so much until my self-esteem soared! I began to swoon from knowing my peers looked up to me and genuinely praised my accomplishment. From that time forward, getting good grades kept others noticing me, at home and at school! Even my parents loved seeing the change.

Before then, I had always been the "little plain Jane" whom no one seemed to notice much. After I began scoring good grades, I quickly wanted to exceed at everything. Too quickly, high grades had become too important to me, and so I set out to prove I could be the best at everything! This soon turned out to be just another spiritual trap to ensnare my immature ego. (Everyone knows ego is just pride, which meant I was heading for a fall). I soon learned, though, even a "fall" could motivate me to change. So, I asked God for His help.

Wisdom Word: Whoever will let go of their limited mindset to catch hold of God's greater vision, can run with it and achieve their piece of His great plan.

CHAPTER TWO

Changing Unlikely Influences

A Zipper

As far back as I can remember I watched my mother sewing things together. Soon I discovered I liked sewing clothes, too. It became therapeutic for me, as I experienced peace and learned patience. Both my father's mother and my mother's mother sewed clothes for us from time to time, and the clothes they produced always fascinated me! For years, I thought my mother's mom had magical powers because the clothes she made for us even had the same scent as readymade clothes. (It was years before I realized a new bolt of fabric from the textile mills had the same smell as readymade clothes because new fabric and the new clothes made from it usually don't require washing prior to sale). As far as I was concerned, Granny's new creations rocked because they even smelled new!

I loved sewing things together to produce something beautiful! Excited, I stayed up late with my mom, intently watching her cut, snip, sew and press different shapes and types of fabric until they became one cohesive unit, forming something beautifully unique! (I now realize God was igniting within me a desire to sew and bring pleasure to others and myself).

We didn't talk much during those late-night escapades; we both quietly focused on the details of what I call "the creative process". Mama was the designer and executor of the process and I was the apprentice. I watched every move she made, and helped wherever she needed me, as every serious apprentice does.

Later, I believed I could launch out a bit further in my sewing projects by making clothes for my dolls. I challenged myself to try new procedures and do some things differently, especially when some of my finished projects failed to function as I had planned. (Such was the case when I forgot to cut an opening in the top of my doll's dress, so her head could get through).

Level 2 was "Home Economics" classes. They excited me because I learned the how-to's of clothing construction. I welcomed each new sewing project with increased anticipation! I seemed to have found my niche, and making pretty things to wear was it!

Soon, I decided to try more home sewing, making more projects like those made at school. At home, I welcomed my oldest sister's help as she showed me how to lay out my pattern pieces on the fabric, interpret the symbols and properly cut them. Later, she even taught me how to insert lining into a garment. (At that time, I could not quite grasp the concept.)

I clearly remember when our Home Economics project was sewing an apron (essential home gear for every aspiring "Baby-Boomer Homemaker"). I was pleased when it turned out better than I thought it would. The following year, a skirt was our project, and the designer/entre-preneur spirit began to stir my heart. I liked sewing clothes because we all needed them. The following year I began making skirts for myself at home, because in a family with three other sisters who swapped clothes, I figured sewing more skirts could help stretch our wardrobe. At the very least, I could add interest to mine.

A few months into making skirts, I got a bright idea: I decided to cut out my skirt and hem it, but I concluded I could wear it sooner if I left off the waist-band and used a safety pin to fasten it. To cover the unfinished waist, I planned to wear longer blouses or tops, and "Voila" I could "rock" my new skirt the next day! (Who would know I had taken a few shortcuts)? Besides, as long as the raw edges didn't show, it really wasn't anyone else's business— or was it?

Shortly afterward, the brilliance on my "bright idea" started to fade. Daddy, who had grown up watching his own mom sew, noticed my shortcuts. He didn't say anything at first, but in his wise and tempered way, he soon announced "a sewing challenge" saying, "I will pay the first person who sews a skirt and completely finishes it, with a zipper to close up the side and a waistband; AND it must have a fastener at the waist."

Well, at the word "pay" my Dad got my attention and pushed my motivation-button. The money would be my very own! As the fourth-born child among five children, I was known as the "knee baby", so I couldn't even remember the last time I had more than two quarters. My brother and sisters usually had no regular money either because there wasn't much money left over for the five of us to have "pocket money". We were not like some kids who received a regular "monetary allowance", so they could learn how to spend money wisely.

I had lofty dreams about the prize money. The very thought of having my *own* money made me feel empowered and influential! Of course, I had no plan for *how* I would spend the money, but just the thought of having it made me feel special. My self-esteem skyrocketed, as I was confident I could rise to Daddy's challenge. I don't recall if my sisters even cared much about it, least of all my brother.

A short time later, I easily won and proudly accepted my prize money (a whopping two dollars, as I recall). While it didn't make me rich, earning it elevated my sense of competence and confidence! I had a fresh perspective of my potential, as I proved I could meet a deadline, *and* produce a garment with an acceptable standard of quality.

Strange, how a "zipper challenge" changed my way of thinking and my self-esteem. It taught me the value of finishing what I start, keeping my word and meeting acceptable standards and deadlines. It created "a sense of balance" for me, jumpstarting my skill building journey, and eventually laying the foundation for my first small business, "Golden ThreadZ". Starting with custom handmade window treatments, it has evolved into a consulting service, providing solutions to enhance and organize home spaces. The business conceived in my spirit during the early years, as I discovered my love for bringing people and their things into order, ease and harmony.

Learning to operate in a broader spectrum of my gift and business even challenged me to change my communication style and discipline my impulsive speech while talking with clients. When excitement tempted me to over-talk people or their issues, or fatigue made me think about "quitting", my "zipper mindset" realigned my attitude. It still ignites me to finish what I've started because quitting is *not* a productive option. Grateful for God's Spirit working through my Dad, motivating me to change, I am indebted to them both for influencing me at such an impressionable time in my life.

Wisdom Word: Don't be so quick to overlook or ignore a small beginning. God is the One who made the mighty oak tree start from a tiny seed. Your seed is within you. Water it every day by reading God's word. Remember to pray for understanding before you read, and start practicing it now. Anyone who sincerely chooses can decide to go the distance, "from seed-sown to seed-grown".

All in the Family

I believe the traditional family unit is the crucible where God ordained us to grow, learn to adapt and mature. In the environment of family, each of us learns (first-hand) the dynamic of people in-relationship, as we discover how to fit into others' lives. There we begin to discover our value. We also experience how to manage emotions and communicate our expectations and disappointments; it's where we learn to speak up for ourselves and grow in our personal relationship with God.

"The family *unit*" also is the principle target of our adversary, the devil. He aims to strike it relentlessly—to confuse, pervert and destroy it! Our family assignment is God's practicum for living in concert with His kingdom standards. The more we learn to live as God planned, the better He trains us to live in unity with the God head. Now, I want to set the stage for you to appreciate my unique family, as I share lessons I learned about choice and change.

We were different in every way: In gender, occupation, conversation, and personality; in body types, shoe sizes, hair types, and blood types; in eye colors, gifts, talents, and skills; food preferences, allergies, backgrounds, education, ad infinitum!

Daddy was born into a small family learning to adjust to urban change. They lived in a Southern state and Daddy grew up the only male child in his family, because his older brother died at ten years old. He never knew his first and oldest sister because she died at birth. This is why he ended up in the position of eldest brother to his younger sister. Once or twice, he admitted to me he always wished his older brother had lived, because he felt uncomfortable trying to fill that role. His family rented a run-down (but neatly kept) house directly across the street from a penitentiary.

Daddy confessed he hated fighting, but if a bully backed him into a corner, he said he learned to reach down for half-a-brick (or whatever was handy), to quickly equalize the situation.

At an early age, he learned to sing well. Both he and his sister learned to play piano. As a gifted portrait and cartoon artist, he preferred to work in charcoals, pastels, oil, and pencils to produce striking portraits and cartoon images. He learned academic subjects easily, graduating early from High School to enroll in a Virginia college on a full scholarship, until the World War II Draft interrupted his education. After the war, he began a thirty-year career with the United States Postal Service, and I never remember a time when Daddy was unemployed. He also worked part time jobs into the wee hours of the morning, as needed.

In his thirties, God called him to preach the Gospel, where during the course of his lifetime, he served as pastor for several churches and attended Bible College.

When undertaking an unfamiliar task or project, he did it "by the book". Whether painting the house, fixing the sump pump, or decorating the Christmas tree, he always checked the instructions first. Daddy loved listening to music, food shopping, and preparing gourmet meals. He specialized in exploring international cuisine, preparing and sampling imported foods. He was a gentle, caring, charismatic man who, though gifted to speak, disliked arguments and confusion, and he never liked administering corporal punishment.

Mama, on the other hand, was born in a different Southern state to rural sharecroppers. She was born on a tenant farm, third from the youngest of ten. She had three brothers, (one of them dying from a birth defect three days after birth), and she had five sisters (with one passing away at ten years old from a weak heart).

At age forty-two, a heart attack stole her father away from them; Mama was between eight and ten years old when it happened. As a result, her family scattered among relatives in other cities and states until they later reunited.

She stayed for a short time with her very tall African grandfather and his wife, before reuniting with her mother and two other siblings.

Following her father's final advice to "always work hard", Mama began working for a Jewish family when she was eleven years old, "for room and board". The couple (a doctor and a lawyer) encouraged her to finish high school, where she met and later married Daddy. Encouraged through Daddy's mentoring, her family's help with childcare, and faithful coaching from one of her most committed instructors (Edna Purdy James), Mama became the only member of her family to graduate from college, as a member of The Medical College of Virginia's first Nursing Class. The following year, our family moved further North to greener pastures.

Adhering to her father's final advice, Mama's work ethic has been firm and forceful. For more than five decades, she worked rotating shifts as a full-time nurse, while managing her most important full-time position, "Homemaker". Later, she would add to those duties, preacher's wife, missionary, and civic worker. She was even an Avon Representative for a while. She was a talented dressmaker, a "down home, hash-slinging country cook" (like "Granny", her mom), and in her retirement years, she even started a home-based catering business called, "Try Something Different". She is known for being a diligent saver and a shrewd financial manager. God gave her profound wisdom and trusted her as an "ever ready giver", whenever He revealed a need.

She regarded herself as a mediocre singer, but sang on many church choirs and, for a time, with a female Gospel group, while juggling her other roles. She accomplished most of this even before learning to drive (at age forty-two).

Above all, she was the quintessential "Champion of the Verbal Comeback", and I always wished I could "fire back" a zinger of a response to people the way she could, and still does. She had no problem using her words to transmit "little motivational reminders" to help us all (including Daddy) stay on track until our tasks were completed.

Mama made sure we all knew the medical names for most of our anatomy, and she let us know we were never to use "street slang" to explain symptoms, even during doctor's visits. Oh, and by the way, all of us knew we must "be a good patient" whenever we saw a doctor, whether Mama was with us nor not. (Even now, I try to represent her well during my doctor visits).

I was honored (and maybe a little too pleased) to volunteer information when Mama and Daddy asked how we enjoyed ourselves during our teenage parties. I especially enjoyed reporting juicy details about who danced too slowly and too closely. My siblings, on the other hand, hated my willingness to "snitch" on them. I'm sure I "earned my stripes" with my parents, but not so much with my brother and sisters. I'm sure they must have considered me "a double agent".

Earlier, I mentioned Daddy's reaction to my birth when he first saw I shared some of his physical traits. Well, apparently, my siblings noticed it, too, and concluded he might have had a soft spot for me. (I really didn't notice him treating me any differently, but apparently they did). After a while, they began using Daddy's regard for me and his dislike for administering corporal correction to their advantage. When getting to the root of disagreements, Daddy preferred using a method he called, "the Army way", to solve issues arising among us children. He especially liked to use this "method of interrogation" to find out "Who-Done-It" when something went wrong or missing.

On one occasion, Daddy suspected one of us of having done something prohibited, but when he lined us up to question us, no one confessed to the wrongdoing. So, he decided *to not* punish any of us (because he couldn't prove who was guilty). This continued to happen until Daddy got wise. One day, someone had "sampled" a little too much from the dinner plate Mama usually set aside for him when he worked late. The culprit had eaten most of his dinner, and she had nothing acceptable to offer him when he came home from work.

Just as before, Daddy questioned all of us, but no one confessed. Then, to our surprise, he punished all of us! From then on, whenever someone was guilty of a serious offense, the older siblings would come to me and say, "Pat, when Daddy asks, "Who did it?" just say you did it, because he won't punish you—you're his favorite." Eager to fit in, I would always end up saying, "I did it, Daddy." I suspect he knew I was lying, but I was surprised when he actually softened his tone and changed his mind about the punishment! My brother and sisters were surprised too, and delighted! After that, when someone slipped up and crossed the line, they would ask me to cover for them by saying I did it. (I don't think they really thought they were "leading me to the proverbial slaughter" because they were so positive Daddy would always change his mind, rather than punish me.)

Oh, but I will never forget the day Daddy got wise to what they were doing. Again, someone had transgressed a serious house rule and Daddy called for an interrogation.

As usual, we staged our normal "defense", but this time was different. Daddy punished me as though I *were* the offender! I will never forget it. In fact, I remember every detail to this day!

I remember how quickly I changed my mind about "helping the team" do wrong. Daddy did not approve of what they had been doing, but he also wanted to teach me a lesson about being a willing accomplice to a lie. I knew I was wrong to do it, and he always wanted to remind me "a lie is still a lie!

No one ever used that strategy again as a way to get away with doing wrong, and I matured in *great* wisdom very quickly as I rapidly changed how I sought to be popular!

God's Unconditional Love

I've learned God invites us into a "family relationship" because He wants to show us how to love Him the way Jesus and the Holy Spirit love Him, and us. Each of us has received His "agape" (the God-kind of love) to extend to everyone we meet who has a love-vacuum. God uses our horizontal relationships within His spiritual family to train and mature us.

We show love for God when we show genuine love to others, though I am the first to admit talking about it is a lot easier than doing it. He has shown me His love is patient *and* kind, especially while I wait for a bad situation to change for the better. His love is NOT jealous, NOT boastful, NOT proud, NOT rude, NOT demanding of its own way and NOT irritable. His love keeps NO record of being wronged, does NOT rejoice over injustice, but rejoices when truth wins out. His love NEVER gives up, NEVER loses faith, is ALWAYS full of hope, and endures throughout EVERY circumstance (principle taken from 1 Corinthians. 13:4-7). God's kind of love is, in fact, "Boots on the Ground".

When God sends His trained and prepared prayer warriors into a fight, it shows we have graduated from "classroom concepts" (learning *about* spiritual tactics and strategies to engage the enemy), to "the spiritual battlefield" (where we actually *use* His spiritual weapons (His Word and His love) to stand our ground. As soldiers in God's army, we must *never* "throw in the towel". We *must* engage our spiritual enemy by staying in the fight to love people unconditionally, as God does. It's hard sometimes, but we *must* constantly remind ourselves that *people* are not our enemy. The one who opposes us is the devil, (Lucifer-now Satan), the ousted archangel Jesus, our Redeemer already defeated at the Cross! We must reset our minds to recall we are already *more than conquerors* because of His victory!

(Our Heavenly Father still hates the sin defiling the lives of the innocent people He created, but He loves the people He made, even though we sin). We must do our best, always, to show God's caliber of love to everyone, and we must do it from the heart.

Unlovely thoughts, unloving attitudes, hateful words and deceitful actions weaken our ability to overcome in the skirmishes the wicked one devises to sabotage our peace and unity. For whatever reasons, when we fail to renew our minds to God's Word, we're slowing the approach to our God-given mission and goal.

We can *choose* to show God's love in many ways, and befriending others is definitely one of those ways. *"When I was a child, I spoke and thought and reasoned as a child, but when I grew up, I put away childish things [speech, thoughts and reasoning]." [Emphasis added]. (I Corinthians 13:11)*

Innocent Love

As far back as I can remember all of us depended on each other, but we mostly depended on our oldest sister, who managed our daily care according to our parents' strict instructions. Her responsibility was to oversee our domestic activities and maintain order in the house. Perhaps the most important aspect of her responsibility was to ensure everything ran smoothly while our parents were at work. The rest of us were more or less compliant, driven by her unusual commitment. She focused on keeping every situation under her firm control and tolerated no rebellion to her delegated authority. Our sibling order made me feel secure for a long time, and I clung, psychologically and socially, to its established codes of conduct. It took years to disengage myself from the need for others' approval, including that of my oldest sister.

I can remember feeling relatively obscure as I started to mature and think for myself. My siblings, on the other hand, appeared to attach no special value to my personal opinions because, after all, I was only "the knee baby". (I didn't know every child yearns for personal acceptance and respect for his or her own uniqueness). Later I would learn how even immature children, eventually, will avail themselves of any opportunity to challenge the status quo to secure their own sense of acceptance.

My Friend

When I was about fourteen, I remember challenging the status quo, by taking advantage of opportunities to visit one of my friends who also sang on our church choir. I sensed this friend (and one or two others) felt marginalized, as I did. In their company, I felt free to express my opinions because they actually "listened" when I talked. Some even asked "my" advice from time to time, and their attention made me feel important and relevant.

Whenever I saw them treated insensitively, I felt drawn to console them, as I did when one friend seemed to need special acceptance. I looked for opportunities to help him in ways that made sense to me at the time. It wasn't long before I began to regard "meddling" in his troubles as "helping".

I decided to keep it "close hold" and not tell my parents this particular friend was a boy my age. I was sure my Mom and Dad would not have approved. They would have considered my action as breaking one of our important household rules: We must be sixteen before we could date (although I didn't consider it dating). I had seen them invoke that rule with my three older siblings. So, even though I knew this friendship was platonic, I suspected my parents would stand on principle. I didn't want to hear that response because my friend seemed needy.

This friend was special. He sang on our church choir and I liked his innocence. I think I most liked his beautiful singing voice, and singing was one of my passions, too! As members of our church's Junior Choir, (and later, as part of a community fellowship choir) we all loved singing and harmonizing together (he, my younger sister and I). Besides, as members of the same church, our families were friendly and, sometimes, we all fellowshipped together. Occasionally they allowed him and me to go for a walk on a Sunday afternoon or spend friend-time, just visiting in the other's home, but always with family members present. During a few of these Sunday afternoon walks he and I enjoyed talking as we strolled past the shops of our community shopping center.

One time as we casually walked and talked, I was shocked when a group of boys our age began to harass him with degrading and inappropriate remarks. I was deeply embarrassed for him and hurt by the ugly things they said. Instinctively, I reached for his hand and held it as we walked past them. (I held his hand because I wanted the bullies to *think* I was his girlfriend, hoping to silence them, or at least make them feel ashamed of their hateful remarks). After the incident, I felt attached to his wounded ego and emotional pain. I began using our friendship to shield him from harassment. This being at the forefront of my thoughts, I always looked for chances to spend time with him, to reinforce our companionship. I thought I was guarding him from alienation and rejection. (I was too naïve to know the danger I could have gotten myself into). All I saw was a friend hurting and no one else seemed to notice or protect his teenage heart from battery.

From then on, if Mama asked me to go to the store for her, I quickly accepted. Then I'd run really fast to the store (in hopes I could redeem a few extra minutes to manage a "detour" to visit his family. After the drop-in visit, I'd run even faster back home, hoping no one had noticed the extra time I had used before returning. (Of course, my parents noticed, but they didn't reveal they knew until it happened too many times for their comfort).

I was not trying to "date" him. I was making a feeble, childish attempt to show loving concern for a friend, someone who seemed to need genuine caring friends. Love protects and love is kind, and I was trying to protect him from the cruelty all of us can sometimes show, when we *convince ourselves* another person is different or when fear, born of our own implicit biases, invades and overtakes what we want to protect as "our own safe space".

Each time I visited his family, I was convinced my friend was just an ordinary, insecure kid, perhaps needing a role model, because his father was not present in their home. Only his mom and grandmother served as authority models at his home. I think it was "innocently natural" for him to grow up handling life situations as he had seen them handled by his two closest adult figures, who just happened to be women. The more I spent time with them, none of his actions or activities led me to think anything was wrong about him or his behavior. My friendship and kindness were all I could provide to reinforce his faith that humans can be kind to one another. However, gossip and presupposition trampled his bruised self-esteem until others' suspicions eventually tarnished his reputation. By the time we graduated high school, I finally accepted I was "not my friend's keeper". I also forced myself to admit I, as friend, could not do what only God (his true Father) and his mom were responsible to do for him.

I finally realized my friend was my friend only—not my responsibility, because I was "not" an adult. I didn't know, then, my responsibility as a believer and friend was to pray for him and show God's love to him, as I exhibited the fruit of the Spirit. Therefore, my loyalty as a friend remained, but my self-assumed role as his "protector" had to stop. My futile attempts to play that role had resulted only in making me feel more helpless, more defeated and more insignificant. I finally changed my mind and admitted his situation was never really "in my lane"; I also began understanding this truth: "Sneaking" to do anything (even something good) is never wise. It only results in exposure, tainted by negative assumptions. Failure to be straightforward and get permission is sneaking, and sneaking reveals the presence of fear and selfishness, which produce dishonesty. At the end of the day, dishonesty breaches trust. And trust, my friends, is *very* difficult to mend.

Years later in my fifties, I stood over my friend's casket looking down at his physical remains. I was surprised how He had changed in the years after we both graduated from the same high school, to pursue our separate destinies. Looking at him that one last time, I realized he was no longer the tender teenager I remembered. Standing there, my heart stopped breaking over his unfortunate childhood. He had grown up and matured, just as I had done. He had chosen to deal with life on his own terms, as I had done. Standing there in silence, I was tempted to grieve again over the assault of ignorance unloving people had perpetrated against his innocence at so young an age. I still struggled to hold back my tears, just as I did when we took those Sunday afternoon walks. As I stood there, I wept inwardly over my friend, and the pure friendship we experienced those many years before. Even though I know I will rejoice again when I see him in Heaven, God seemed to have been saying to me, as I gazed at his body, "Pat, you can stop hurting for him, now. I had him covered all the days of his life, and I've got him covered now."

As for those bullies and accusers, God loves them, too, with an everlasting love and underneath them (and me, and you) are His everlasting arms! I have forgiven them of their cruelty, their insensitivity and maybe even fear, because I too have been cruel and fearful, and God forgave me. I forgive them because unconditional love demands it—and ultimately, I do it because I must freely give what I have so freely received from God.

A Message from Maturity: Stop "Helping" God

As I remember my perceived need for others' approval and my failed attempts to get that approval on my own, I pause. I try to be watchful for the frailty of my own limited wisdom (called "devilish wisdom" in James 3:15) as it still tries to sneak in and infiltrate my thoughts sometimes. It wants my will to declare mutiny to God's will and, thereby, try to override God's wisdom. Sometimes, it still feels risky to step out of the shadows of fear and self-doubt to express my own deeply held beliefs, especially with non-family members. However, I am learning I do not have the power to force people to agree with my opinion. Even when they disagree, it's okay. They have their will and opinions and I have mine. Actually, I guess things should be this way, because God created all of us as unique persons. I'm learning only God needs to approve of my motives and actions. Other people are not qualified to do so, since they too are subject to human frailty.

I know from reading my Bible God wants us to be "in unity on the things that matter to Him". My friend mattered to Him. I matter to Him. Every person matters to Him. So, the one way we can be unified is to believe in the God who created us and the world, and to respect the high, matchless price He paid to make it possible for us to choose to show love to everyone, regardless of our differences. When we accept God's message of unconditional love, which came through Jesus Christ's ransomed blood at Calvary, we enter common ground with all humanity as we live to love. I am learning I cannot remain stuck in a cocoon shielding me from embracing others, along with their differences. I must strive to be fearless because real love requires it! Real love is fearless because real love is a Person, Jesus Christ, the Suffering Servant! As I continue loving others, despite the scratches, bruises and sometimes wounds of close encounters, the more I grow to be more like Him.

CHAPTER THREE

Choosing New Hopes And Dreams

"Feelings are like dreams; you have to examine them to see where they're coming from (and where they're going), before believing or accepting them."

Feelings are the guideposts of relationships, and the thermometers of change; they can indicate where you are, but not necessarily which way to go. So, beware of "feeling your way" through life.

When I decided to marry because my high school "best friends" had married, I short-circuited my hopes and dreams. I thank God He holds my future, and He worked my foolish decisions into His plan (to mature me and help me develop grit—the stuff on which strong relationships thrive). If God didn't rescue me from the vain things for which I hoped and dreamt, I would have self-destructed! When I launched out in my own arrogance, I paid a high price for being dishonest to myself and to others.

Starting College

"Starting" college was easier than doing the hard work (academically and emotionally) to stay there until I finished. Growing up, I had been sheltered and given small responsibilities, which failed to prepare me to face the rigors of deeper commitments. Registering for classes, buying books and obligating my future to indebtedness was easy enough to do. Beyond that, I would need to build my life around the practice of proven wisdom to accomplish my new goals. My high school life had never really demanded serious commitment from me, so I never regarded myself (or any job I did) as important. College life was riskier, and completely different than I had expected. I felt alienated as I overheard conversations in the break rooms. I was shocked when students shamelessly discussed their plans to have abortions the same way they planned to change their clothes or makeup. I was comfortable being around my church Buddies, who at least, seemed to have a conscience about such things.

Many things were different, as I tried to adjust to the "college atmosphere". I was free now to make my own choices, and I found myself choosing to give in to laziness and skip the classes that challenged me to work and think hard. Bluntly speaking, I couldn't handle the freedom. I actually felt lost without someone older telling me what to do or expect next. Lack of self-discipline was sabotaging my hopes and dreams, draining my motivation. I didn't know how to harness what was out of control and make things work for my good. I wasn't used to working hard and steady for long periods, or working things out for myself. I was accustomed to doing only what was easy, or what siblings directed me to do.

When the possibility of marriage popped up on my horizon, I dropped out of my boring studies to walk down the aisle and say, "I Do" because it was easier. *Starting* college had been easy, too, so I had to ask myself, "Why did you fail to finish what you started there?"

The devil's greatest seduction is "enticing" each of us to *disregard* our "intermittent due seasons" and miss the "fullness of time appointment" when it comes. (Read Ecclesiastes, Chapter 3) The seasons of my life had become hopelessly confused and dead-ended.

Fear of failure still wrestled to gain the upper hand in my mind taunting, "You have already failed, and all your paradigms for succeeding at life and marriage have suddenly shifted." The fairy tale future I had expected faded into a heavy fog. (I didn't know the root cause of it was tied to neglecting my time with God to find His wisdom for this part of my life).

Marriage in the Crosshairs

Interwoven with my fear and youthful indecision was a life altering factor I, nor anyone else, anticipated. It was the Vietnam War. When I look back at how it changed our daily living, I am amazed our marriage survived as long as it did.

The war prevented my small family from sharing important life events, making it next to impossible to bond as a couple and a family. We had been married for only one month before my husband went to Southeast Asia as part of the Army infantry, on the front lines of the war. Of course, I worried all the time he might never return, and it ramped up my fear to new levels. In the seven years our marriage lasted, we rarely spent more than thirty consecutive days together between his rotations; the longest rotation was eighteen months. Within our first eighteen months, we shared the joy (and responsibility) for our son and daughter, with just a few months to do that together. Then, when our daughter was only four months old, I had to return to work full-time or I would have lost my job, due to insufficient seniority. I have always regretted that decision, because she and I had so little time to bond.

More Challenges

Whenever my husband was home for fewer than thirty days, I found it difficult to relinquish control of our established order and domestic routine, because the children and I had become so accustomed to "my way" of parenting. His assignments rarely gave us the option to live under one roof long enough to build a strong family unit. As two nineteen-year-olds, neither of us had grown in grace and wisdom enough to avoid the demonic traps set for us. Our lives were shifting in unimaginable ways; still God used what seemed like a setback, to setup and reset our lives to work all our mistakes together for good. He never left us, even though we ended up leaving each other.

Within the fifteen years after our divorce, (older but not much wiser), we both would decide to remarry. Though my reasons would be different, regrettably, I got the same outcome as before. I was older, but still prideful and spiritually immature. Thankfully, as I watched other couples fight the good fight, I eventually learned a good marriage is a result of *faithfully* doing the hard, mundane stuff—the work of loving unselfishly and unconditionally. Now, I am thankful for daily examples and opportunities teaching me how God loves through people.

Pride Blinds and Cripples Relationships

"...It is easy to think that we "know" over problems like this, but we should remember that while this "knowing" may make a man look big, it is only love that can make him grow to his full stature. For if a man thinks he "knows", he may still be quite ignorant of what he ought to know. But if he loves God, he is the man who is known to God. (I Corinthians 8:1(b), J. B. Phillips). Another translation finishes this verse, *"opening his whole life to the Spirit of God."*

In relationships, I believe many opportunities arise for pride to sneak in and blind the minds of everyone involved. You see, pride is more than emotion. When we choose to believe otherwise, we deceive ourselves. Pride is a contaminating spirit specializing in mutiny (the overthrow of order and authority for ruin and selfish gain).

Pride and arrogance are demonic agents sent to cripple our relationships, especially the institution of marriage. I learned how they can transform, and speak to me as if I were talking to myself, so I didn't always recognize when my thoughts were infected by their poison. Any environment of unity, harmony, happiness and love is an "antihistamine" to evil influences.

The Bible teaches that the devil interjected pride into the human mind through his suggestions in the Garden of Eden because he was, and is, seeking to blind all humanity with deception. (He is deceived and still wants to replace God, to receive worship from humans). Be aware of his devices! I told myself, "Pat, the devil's strength *is* his deception. His goal is to magnify your weaknesses to the point where they're all you focus on. Then he will blindside you to make you want to "over compensate" in your areas of strength to atone for those weaknesses." (He knows that inappropriately using your strengths can render them ineffective). He wanted me confused! He also wanted me to think I should try to "redeem my own failures". God wants us to know every person has weaknesses, so we all need *His* strength and redemption. He inspired the Apostle Paul to write, *"...God has given me grace to speak a warning about pride. I would ask each of you to be emptied of self-promotion and not create a false image of your importance. Instead, honestly assess your worth by using your God-given faith as the standard of measurement, and then you will see your true value with an appropriate self-esteem." (Romans 12:3 TPT)*

In Retrospect: I spent far too many of my childhood years comfortably indoors, avoiding normal challenges and skirmishes. I dreamed and wished a lot, instead of engaging and discovering new people, new conflicts, new horizons and outcomes. I suspect some of you still do it, too. Though we matured in some ways, we still can be slow to step into the unknown, engage the unexpected and master it. Whatever we do, IF we want to change, we *must* choose to keep engaging to persevere!

CHAPTER FOUR

Choosing To Move Upward

Changing Directions

When I became uncomfortable with where and how I lived, I felt like God was "hissing" for me to move; it would be to a place where He would reform my life. I didn't know He had reform in mind as I began focusing on finding a new place to live and a better job. (I had expected to be living more comfortably in my "fantasy life" by now, but instead I lived from paycheck to paycheck). I also needed a reliable vehicle to drive, but instead, I was leaving home at 4 o'clock in the morning to take a bus to a job over twenty-five miles away. There were times when I prayed as I double-locked my door, whispering, "God, please keep my children safe while I'm at work" because I had no reliable babysitter and no more leave left to request. Gradually, I learned to conserve my leave, by going to work whether or not I felt like it, and this discipline rewarded me greatly, the longer I worked.

Thankfully, God stepped in and made a way of escape for me. He caused compassion to overflow my mother's heart, and through her, I received a brand-new vehicle! To this day, I thank God for my mother's obedience to give to needy situations. The ministries of helping and giving have seemed to come naturally to her, but maybe she compassionately remembered her tough beginnings, causing her to identify with my struggle.

Changing Destination

My decision to move set in motion a new series of events affecting every facet of how I would live from then on. This relocation was signaling a new chapter of my life I didn't know would span the next three decades—and beyond. This move was about to change my definition of culture, of family, of economics, of priorities, of religion, of relationship, of politics—everything! For me, this change meant choosing to "do" something different. Did it look strange? Yes. Did it feel strange? You can bet good money it did!

At every turn, I found myself struggling to make the right decisions. Other changes gradually became clearer, although my path still looked pretty narrow and rocky, with no clear stretch of road to follow and catch my breath for a while.

Overwhelmed by so many changes in so many ways, my stress level was off the charts—again! In all this, I knew one thing for sure: I was the one ultimately responsible for my own failure or success, and unless I chose to do something about it, no one else could do it for me. It forced me to break away from the lazy habit of expecting others to do for me what I should (and could) do for myself.

So I got moving on a plan to relocate far from relatives and friends, leaving the fast pace of city life to be nearer to my workplace. On the advice of a wise friend, I moved my children away from the toxic city, with its stacked high-rise apartments, which did not work for us. Something deep in me yearned for "green space" and a slower pace, which I found in the county near my job. Its slower pace fit my slow, laid-back personality much better.

Changing Socially and Spiritually

Changing the direction of our lives involved new ways of thinking and acting, if we were to survive. As soon as I began home hunting, I encountered people who had their own ideas about what "they thought" I deserved in a place to live. What they showed me differed greatly from my expectations. Rental agents showed me worse places than I had lived in the city! Growing weary of "hoping" for their compassion and trying to "be nice", I finally spoke up, assertively, saying, "I'm sorry, but I need a place located in the front of the community, where the grass is thick and green. I had more grass in the city than what you're showing me here!" After I was frank about my preferences, the agent showed me several townhomes, from which I selected one in the first court near the community's entrance. I lived there for more than ten years, and I thank God for giving me boldness to speak my mind politely.

Changing directions involved speaking up for my children too. It meant modeling patience in spite of demeaning comments from others who regarded themselves as having a "better standard of living". Gradually, I did change my standard of living (by changing my thinking and some of my friends). God's Holy Spirit began leading me to people and situations that encouraged me to keep going upward toward His right standard. I eventually rededicated my life to Christ and committed my daily living to being more Christ-like. As I called to God for help, He faithfully responded. The God of my childhood was still "there" with me and for me. He was wooing me to continue in the place of peace I had known with Him. Years later, I learned one of God's redemptive names is, "The Lord is There"! He promised to "never leave nor forsake me" and He did not! He waited years for the moment I would choose to return my attention to Him, and spend more time with Him willingly. In a reunion of sweeter fellowship and divine communication, The Lord, My Shepherd was there, providing everything I needed, especially His wise counsel.

Sanctifying My Speech

When God invites His children to return to right fellowship with Him, He sets us apart as holy, through the indwelling of His Holy Spirit. He wants us to fellowship in a holy atmosphere. He wants every part of our body, including the tongue, to serve His holy purposes.

I don't recall learning this after I first asked Jesus Christ to be Lord of my life. I do remember my parents saying Jesus wanted us to live our lives to reflect His character, but I didn't know it meant using His gifts and talents exclusively for His purposes. He calls this "consecration to holiness". Unaware He had set me apart from the "practice" of sin my mind was constantly fighting between Bible standards of living and the popular culture's standard of living. So I learned some vain things. Among other gifts, God gave me a mouth and words to express love and appreciation *to* Him and *for* Him. Never did I think I would ever use my mouth to speak words that grieved His Holy Spirit living in me. Before long, I discovered ignorance, pride, and foolishness really do bind themselves together in the hearts of children and young adults. It's a volatile mix, which when detonated, scatters our own hopes and dreams, (and those of our parents). Unknowingly, I was searing my conscience, and turning the climate of my soul into one of grief for God's Holy Spirit to live in.

I knew I must learn to slow down and cooperate with God's Spirit, and let Him teach me His ways to change my habits for His good service. Exhausted, I discovered I could not do it on my own, and thankfully, God, my Sanctifier patiently helped me change my ways. However, one thing He could not (and would not) do for me—"choose".

As mentioned earlier, not knowing how to handle feelings of insecurity during my early years had sparked a constant need to feel perfect. I thought I could display self-confidence by projecting a strong outer-image to attract friends, but that was fake, transparent to anyone who really listened. With every task, came a mask, and an insatiable need to be perfect in every detail, because I thought, "the more I impress others, the more they will love and accept me." Afraid to fall short of others' expectations, I sometimes made unacceptable choices, hoping those I admired would include me in their circle of friends. It even happened with family members. I wanted to prove I could measure up to their standards too; or maybe I should say "measure down" in this case.

I made one of those "unacceptable choices" when I chose to punctuate my speech with profanities to "sound cool" like those whom I regarded as strong and savvy. Well, the more I laced my vocabulary with toxic words, the more polluted my mind and heart became. (I didn't always understand the spiritual connection, but in my heart I knew my words were not acceptable, especially since my parents never permitted "smutty language" in our home.

After moving into my first apartment, my standards slipped lower and pride seduced me to live whatever way I chose because after all, it was "my place" and at last, "I" was finally an independent adult. (How quickly I'd forgotten I was also mother of two other little lives).

By now, I was working the graveyard shift because it paid more, but it also brought opportunities to burn the candle of my life at both ends, and my ability to make right choices suffered. My job involved backbreaking heavy lifting, but I was young, so I figured I could handle it. Physically, it may have strengthened my lower back and calves, but socially it only enhanced my love of talking and being the center of attention.

Proverbs 18:21 (TPT) says, *"Your words are so powerful that they will kill or give life, and the talkative person will reap the consequences.*

I had not been reading my Bible regularly, and I began sliding down a slippery slope as I stopped surrounding myself with godly friends. One night at work, I was the center of attention, "weaving an exciting verbal account" (exaggerating an event) as coworkers stood around listening. I didn't realize I was using more profanity than usual until a male coworker, whose conversations were usually full of low-life imagery and profanity, quietly approached me and asked, "Does it take all that to make your point?" He was referring to the barrage of dirty words I had been using. Apparently, the profanity had managed to offend even him!

I pretended to brush off his comment like it didn't matter, but deep inside I was convicted in my backslidden soul. I felt degraded because my habit of dirty speaking had gotten so far out of line it had even offended someone I thought was morally below me! That coworker might not have realized it, but God had used him, (a heathen) to correct my foolish misconduct! Instantly I knew it was really God correcting me! The time had come for me to STOP IT! I was not modeling the habits of Christ or the behavior my parents had trained me to reflect. I had sullied God's reputation and compromised His righteous standard! I knew in my heart of hearts that God was not pleased; my conduct was keeping someone else from embracing His good plan for their life.

My habit didn't disappear right away, but when the Holy Spirit convicted me of sin, I *wanted* to start changing my words. Once my will changed, the rest was a matter of time.

"Sanctification" means purification and freedom from *practicing* sin. I started changing when I *decided* to agree with God that my speech would conform to His holy standard. I asked Him to help because I knew I was powerless to help myself.

For more than thirty years now, I have rejected toxic words and chosen healthy words, to avoid offending the sensibilities of others. I am grateful my Heavenly Father, still cares enough to train me up in the way I *should* go. I'm finally free of that nasty habit and I try hard to constantly forgive others who still choose to spread what I label "noise pollution" with their words. God, also, is working on their will to display the profitable gift of wholesome words available to them. I'm glad I chose to change my words; life-filled words leave a wholesome legacy for others to imitate.

The Takeaway: Remember Jesus' reminder when He said, "But I tell you, on the day of judgment people will have to give an accounting for every careless or useless word they speak. For by your words [reflecting your spiritual condition] you will be justified and acquitted of the guilt of sin; and by your words [rejecting Me] you will be condemned and sentenced. (Matthew 12:36 AMP) That's why we should confess new sins daily.

Finishing College

In Chapter 3, I mentioned how I failed to follow through with my commitment to finish college after high school. I dropped out when I was only a month shy of finishing my first academic year. As I recall, I really didn't want to go to the Teacher's College where I had enrolled. My parents had made the decision for me when they "announced" the news to me. I remember they explained they wanted me to take advantage of a special program for high school graduates, called the "Teacher's Pledge Program". It offered high school graduates a four-year teacher's education if they signed an agreement to teach, in state, for two years following their graduation. I liked the thought of teaching, but I was not thrilled to learn I would be going to college in the same state where I went to high school.

I thought attending college meant living *away* from home. My heart hit the floor as I realized I'd be riding the same city bus that transported me to high school, then returning home to do housework and homework, just as I did in high school. (I wished I knew then how life is all those mundane things). I had seen movies on TV showing how some kids "lived the college life" and I wanted to experience that excitement! Every time I thought about waiting at the "same" bus stop, to ride to another part of the "same" city for college, my expectations shifted to "idle".

Of course, young people of my era, (so-called "Baby Boomers") did not "talk back" to our parents, especially when their decision was firm. I feebly tried explaining my college expectations, but I was too timid to negotiate with my parents. I could see their resolve was firmly set, so I pretended to agree, to avoid a conflict of opinions.

After thinking it over, I did accept their logic, since I was not the one paying for my education. I decided I would gratefully accept the offer my parents could afford.

What I *thought* I wanted was freedom to satisfy my emotional and social needs. I also secretly relished the bonus of being free from going to church all the time! Though I would never have admitted it openly, I longed to be free from following those old home rules, and free from the ever-watchful eyes of my parents. (What a foolish, young heart I possessed back then). Of course, I thought I was right, as all young people think. I thought, "Surely I know what I want better than my parents." After all, I was eighteen and fully grown, right? Looking back, I'm not sure I had ANY spiritual wisdom at that time. I didn't even have what city dwellers call "street smarts".

In the end, I did go to the in-state Teachers College they chose, but once enrolled, I chose only to go to the classes I liked. If a subject challenged me to focus too long or study too hard, I procrastinated. I told myself (and believed my own lie) I would "do it later". I hadn't yet learned the raw truth that "procrastination is a child of laziness". Instead, I fantasized I was a bright and bold rising star, outshining most of my peers. I didn't know arrogance had puffed up my ego and blinded me. Neither did I know I was in a "denial-mindset".

After only seven months, I didn't bother to formally withdraw from my courses. Once again, I had taken what I thought was the "easy" way out and had run from the challenge. In my mental fantasy, I guess I thought the mess I was creating would simply disappear, or someone else would clean it up, as they did when I was younger.

By this time, I realized marriage had not worked for me, and I felt like a failure.

(If I had slowed down and learned some self-discipline while in college the first time, it might have strengthened some good spiritual habit in me, which could have helped me handle the institution of marriage better than I did).

Hindsight Wisdom: This is what I know now: Each previous phase of my life was a stepping-stone to prepare me for a more complex stage of relationship growth. Later, as I submitted resumes for employment, I discovered that showing I completed only *one* year at a four-year college actually confirmed I had *failed to complete* the three remaining years of the program, and my final grades of "Incomplete" did not impress anyone, either.

Reality Check

After dropping out of college, I worked as a substitute teacher at local public schools. During that time, I encountered many of my former high school classmates who had graduated teachers' college by way of the Teachers Pledge Program. They had finished, but I had not. I was learning that dropping out of anything constructive sets a dangerous precedent for dropping out of life. I didn't know then that the effects of missed opportunities would catch up with me and demand a showdown. Neither did I know God was patiently waiting for me to change my mind and stop rejecting His will for my life. The closer I came to age thirty, the more I felt deep disappointment about opportunities I had missed. I needed to feel closure about something—*anything*.

I wanted to go back and finish something! My marriage had fizzled out in divorce and my spouse had remarried, so, my children and I accepted the finality of that closed door. As I reflected on other broken commitments, including my stalled career, I became desperate to go back and FINISH SOMETHING! I felt like a failure, and failing was never acceptable!

Maybe I had matured a little, but I think I needed to prove to myself I could aim at a target and strike it, as I had done when I accepted my father's zipper challenge. Eventually, I decided there *was* something I could go back and finish; it was my college degree. I believe God had been the first to put the desire in my heart to go to college, and He was redirecting me back toward the path He had chosen for me.

Soon, new people began "popping into" my life. One of them had information about a college I could attend in the evenings, and even accompanied me through the registration process. God also gave me favor with instructors, who held me accountable to my commitment to complete the required work. In my final year, it seemed almost by chance I ran into one of my first-year professors. We chatted briefly, and he asked if I was nearing time to graduate. (It was already April). I answered, "Well, I'm actually thinking I won't be ready to graduate until September because I owe three end-of-term essays, and I've not even begun to write them." Without realizing it, I had stepped backward onto the treadmill of excuses and procrastination, which usually lead to lateness, and eventually to failure.

I believe God put favor and compassion into this Jewish professor's heart to help me in my dilemma. I believe Professor Al Bedell said what he said and did what he did, in accordance with God's divine plan for this young, foolish, struggling student of a different age, gender, race, ethnicity and work ethic than himself. Gently, he said, "Write the three overdue term papers and bring them to me." I'll review and submit them for you." I can't even begin to express what his decision to intervene meant to me!

God had given me ability and potential before I was born. Only God knew, however, I needed another human being to *believe* in me! I needed a *human* coach to encourage me! I needed God to show up with His unprecedented favor that moves the hearts of mortals. I needed "love with skin on it". God had shifted paradigms, causing the impossible to become possible!

A decade earlier, I had naively closed off my heart from relationships because I had learned the hard way, they could cost more than I was willing to invest, in time, in patience and hard work. I remember thinking, "Bought learning is not so bad, as long as you don't pay too dear for it." Right then I knew I would have to pay the high cost of commitment, one way or the other.

Slowly and tediously, I learned relationships are of paramount importance to God; an essential part of His master plan for all people because He uses others, in community, to help us get to places we could never arrive at on our own.

I still savor the sweetness of celebrating with my family and four of my closest friends who were present on that June graduation day. Graduating meant I had gripped the courage, tenacity and maturity to, FINALLY, set an important, life-changing goal, and *achieve* it.

Wisdom Word: Forget all that is behind and press toward the mark. Do it for the prize of reaching your high calling in Christ Jesus! Anyone can persevere to the finish line, when he or she is willing to change and do the hard work that "finishing" requires.

The Process of Learning Humility

Harboring pride is counterproductive. Doing so tarnished my reputation for a time, revealing the selfishness I'd tried to cover up. It took me a long time to change my mind and "humble myself" before God, or face Divine correction as *He* humbled *me*. I thank God humility shifted into gear when pride made me stumble and fall. Humility was a cleansing agent because of its powerful neutralizing effect. God's Holy Spirit has continued erasing and displacing pride, as I repented of it. We know pride is deceptive and evil, lurking somewhere behind our other temperaments, watching for opportunities to grab the limelight.

Scripture records how Jesus handled demonic solicitations to react proudly. First, He ignored strong appeals to satisfy His fleshly cravings, by focusing on His Heavenly Father's Word and mission. This is how He avoided detours through "Pride-land". Next, He responded to each evil temptation by *saying what His Father said*, which is how He overcame the Tempter. I finally realized I must use that same strategy to resist becoming servant to a spirit of pride. We can become a servant to whomever (and whatever) we yield ourselves to obey. (See Romans 6:16) I knew, then, I would need to practice more of God's Truth.

Typing Flashback

When I was in ninth grade, everyone learned to type. (Now it's called "keyboarding"). I learned by placing my fingers on the "home keys" of a typewriter and striking letters needed to spell any word I wanted to type. Above and below the home keys were more easy-to-reach keys with different letters, to form more words. If this sounds complex, I agree. However, experts guaranteed this method could help us type much faster!

(At the beginning of this book, you might recall I said I was a little slow in doing most things. If an action required any sort of advanced motor skill, I could do it but I was only comfortable doing it s-l-o-w). When typing, I'd rev up my resolve and force my mind and fingers to act as one. Result: I passed my high school final exams in typing (barely), but hey, passing is passing!

I thought typing was a mundane skill I'd probably never need because I'd planned to go to college. When I was in high school, the "academic curriculum" was for students planning to go on to college to choose a profession. (The ugly truth was I considered students planning to follow "the business curriculum" low achievers). I know, I know. I mistakenly thought getting higher grades automatically meant I was smarter or better. I also thought a college degree would make me more successful than people specializing in "other" curricula. Gee, did the billionaire dropouts and high school entrepreneurs blow up that theory!

That scenario is an example of pride in its "seed years". However, pride didn't stop there. It planned to grow, by continually enticing me to think proud thoughts and do wrong things until I destroyed myself. The Bible says sin secretly grows from stage one (temptation) to end stage (maturity and death): death of a marriage, a dream, a hope, any good aspiration. The Apostle James wrote by the Holy Spirit, *"Temptation comes from our own desires, which entice and drag us away. These desires give birth to sinful actions. And when sin is allowed to grow, it gives birth to death." (James 1:14-15, NLT)* Thank God for correction!

When I accepted a clerical job, God subjected me to more of His "process of humility". Though I completed college, my ability to type was what actually helped me meet federal job requirements. A few years later when the computer age sprang upon us, I was pleased I had learned to use the keyboard.

I had yearned to use the computer, too, with all its fascinating features, but I just couldn't make myself ask for help; all I needed was the right person to show me how. I had completed a few on-the-job computer classes, but I needed someone to explain "the logic driving the machine". I hadn't asked for help because fear and pride always got in my way. Somehow, I thought I should already know how to use a computer because I could type. I didn't know using a computer was actually more advanced than using a typewriter. I didn't want help from a clerk because it might imply I was deficient. I pushed through each day, handicapped, until I finally gave in and prayed, "God, help me learn the computer."

Up to then I had drafted correspondence by hand, using a "first draft". Office protocol required a clerk to type my "draft" letter in the proper format and return it for me to review and edit, if needed. If my first draft checked out okay, the clerk would mail it. If not, the draft went back and forth!

A few days after I asked God to help me, I asked our office clerk, "Would you type a letter I need? I gave her my draft and told her when I needed it back but her response shocked me when she calmly said, "No I won't." I guess the expression on my face reflected my mixed emotions: shock, surprise, annoyance. Then immediately afterward, with a soft chuckle and a twinkle in her eye she added, "I won't type it, but I'll show you how." As I looked at her, I saw (and felt) the love of God, both in her heart and in the room. He had caused her to answer in a way I would recognize as His answer to my prayer! (This experience reminds me of what Jesus did when He talked with the two disciples on the road to Emmaus after His resurrection. At first, they did not recognize Him. Oh, but later, after they realized it had been their Lord talking with them, they rejoiced)!

My Heavenly Father had been at work answering my prayer. He wanted to teach me how to use the computer and He wanted to teach me humility, so He chose the perfect laborer to do both! (There was no way our clerk had known what I had asked God. You see, I already knew the keyboard, but pride had puffed me up to think, "If I use a 'lowly computer keyboard', my so-called "office status" will be compromised." Typewriters were phasing out, and I'd even seen some executive level employees retire because they refused to learn and use what they considered "a lowly keyboard". (I wonder if God had been presenting them an opportunity to BE humble as they learned to use a computer. I wonder if they were afraid of what "changing" might require of them. I wonder if some did seize the opportunity. Progress was fast overtaking us and God knew I'd let pride prevent me from embracing skills to move me forward. I'm so glad He answered my cry for help and displaced the lie that "I was too important" to ask for help. Only after my distorted self-image came crashing down did I discover God's Holy Spirit right there, replacing my reluctance with zeal, as I left my problem with Him! He's still teaching me to spit out (not swallow) pride, since it has no place in my mind, no business in my actions and no power against my will!

"Lift yourself up with pride and you will soon be brought low, but a meek and humble spirit will add to your honor." (Proverbs 29:23 TPT)

The Takeaway: God uniquely teaches each of His children because He knows each of us brings special value and dignity to whatever He has called us to be and do. Whatever that is, we can be sure it's purpose is always intended for the greater good!

CHAPTER FIVE

Choosing Essentials

A Milestone Restoration

As a "preacher's kid", all I remember was going to church. Whenever I overheard someone say they could "remember their day", a creeping worry would arrest me. I think it troubled me because I couldn't remember the actual day or situation surrounding the first time *I decided* to make a public heartfelt decision to surrender control of my life to Christ.

I do remember walking to the front of our home church when I was about ten years old. I felt pressed to do it because my father had begun talking to my younger sister about something he called "getting saved". I overheard everything he'd been saying to her and I knew, deep down, he had been directing a message toward me too. I was not yet willing to decide, but I knew Daddy was not going to let up until my sister and I both "walked that aisle" and gave our hearts to Christ. He believed his timing was accurate, so he kept the counsel coming our way. I surrendered to end his persistent nudging, but it only secured a temporary peace (as in a "cease fire"). At last, I thought I'd succeeded when he stopped his persuading, thinking I'd gone to the altar of my own free will. I had been deceitful, I know, but the child in me was too timid to stand up under the weight of my father's God-given "Dad-authority". I believed he was probably right in what he'd been saying, but I felt strongly (maybe even defiantly) I did not want to make that decision yet.

As a result, I grew into my teens *hoping* I belonged to Christ without really knowing for sure; I also was embarrassed to admit to anyone that I, a "P. K.", did not know for sure when I surrendered my life to Christ. Even after receiving water baptism at age twelve, I still felt unsure of my conversion. Up to then, my life consisted of regular church going and trying to do what I thought was good by the power of my own will. However, every time I failed to do something I knew God had commanded, I felt like I'd failed God. Eventually many foolish choices made me feel more like a counterfeit, living in secret doubt and (who knows) maybe even a counterfeit heart conversion.

Fast-forwarding to My Mid-Twenties

I finally did experience a powerful encounter with Jesus, that caused me to find my Heavenly Father, and discover the God of all peace. Though He created the universe, His consuming peace confirmed He is my real and personal Father, everywhere present at once!

My Encounter

Lying on my bed with tears tricking down my face, my heart felt crushed. I felt I would surely die from the emotional pain of a broken relationship. I can't remember exactly how long I'd been lying there, but in the midst of tears, I experienced "a sudden knowing" from a source deep within me. I felt "convinced" I should ask God to rescue me from the unbearable pain of this heartbreak. I believed He *could* help me, but I refused to ask for the help I craved because my own disobedience had caused my pain. In stubbornness I thought, "I will NOT ask God for anything because this is what I deserve!" Setting myself as judge, jury and executioner, my flawed reasoning suggested that because I caused the problem, I should also suffer the consequences. I continued to tell myself, "After all, Pat, you're a 'preacher's kid' and surely you know right from wrong."

In spite of the warped counsel coming from my confused conscience, I still felt a continual stronger tugging, and a profound "knowing" that I should cry out to God to deliver me from this mess of jumbled, suffocating feelings I was struggling against. Finally, preparing to silence the "incessant urging" within my spirit, I decided to open my mouth just once, to tell God I would NOT ask Him for help because I did not deserve it; because I did not "feel" worthy.

Just as I opened my mouth to address Him, saying, "Lord...," I suddenly experienced something glorious, like a "giant scroll of peace" slowly unrolling downward over me like an eraser, passing slowly from my head to my feet! As the reality of God's comforting presence and peace flowed over me, my tears instantly dried up from their source. I even forgot the reason for my grief! Instantly, my heart was happy and full of joy! All my anxieties had vanished—GONE in a moment! I began to sob, gratefully, as I supernaturally understood that JESUS NEVER WANTED me to hurt another or be hurt. He NEVER wanted me to act as judge, jury and executioner regarding the consequences of my sins, because He had already shed His sinless blood to eradicate them forever—no matter how vile! I only needed to ASK Him to intervene.

Miraculously, I began to understand my own will had been blocking me from experiencing the joy of accepting complete forgiveness and reconciliation to God! I had wanted a change, but I wanted it my way, which led further away from the transforming power of God. (God will only do in my life what I am willing to let Him accomplish through me). In one gesture of infinite love, His gentle voice had scrubbed emotional stains from my heart, making it completely clean as I submitted my burden to His strong capable hands! I was free from the heavy weight of guilt, and you know what? Now I can remember "my day"!

Wisdom Word: Jesus, our Redeemer, is constantly in the process of changing lives, but you must choose to want what He wants for you. You can ask Him to help you continue changing your mind, so you can be willing and free. Simply ask God, "Lord, help me to want what You want" (as I finally did). Ask Him to help you change your desires, so you can want to welcome His love again. He always wants unblocked relationship with you, but He will never violate your free will; it's His gift to you.

His Advice: "Choose life, so you and your descendants may live: by loving the LORD your God, by obeying His voice, and by holding closely to Him; for He is your life [your good life, your fulfillment] and the length of your days, that you may live in the land which the LORD promised (swore) to give to your fathers, to Abraham, Isaac, and Jacob." (See Deuteronomy 30:15 AMP)

Rededication

If you want to live closer to God, you can do so by asking Him to fill you with His Holy Spirit. Then, *choose* to let His Holy Spirit guide your decisions, your speech and your actions, as you follow His instructions.

Flashback: While carrying my son, I wanted God to give me the gift of His Holy Spirit with the evidence of speaking in languages I never learned (other tongues). So I visited the church of a local pastor and evangelist, and after some instructions on how to "yield" to God's Spirit, I received the infilling of His "Gift" from Heaven. I knew God had filled me with His precious Spirit because after I asked Him for the gift, I spoke in languages I never learned as I rejoiced in Him. I felt incredibly amazed and ecstatic at once! Unfortunately, I did not learn "the value" of having and using this amazing gift, so eventually, I neglected speaking in tongues (using the heavenly language of tongues) to speak to God in prayer.

Back in my normal routine, I "didn't always *feel* like" I still had God's Spirit indwelling me. I didn't know I could (or even should) use my new gift outside the church building. I usually read my Bible at church. Sometimes the sermons might (or might not) instruct me further on the subject of the Holy Spirit.

(Even now as I'm writing, the Holy Spirit is telling me I could not properly use what I was ignorant of). Now I see the more I would have studied and learned *about* the Person of the Holy Spirit, who He is, where He lives and what He does in and through me), my spiritual growth could have been faster. I also know I could have avoided many wrong choices.

Of course, the devil also "read my behavior" and planned strategic decoys for me. Whenever I dismissed wise counsel or followed foolish advice, my life got harder and I became bitter. I even resented people working hard to keep their relationships on course. My darkened mindset began contaminating other relationships; I was a social and emotional "train wreck". How messed up was that! However, God's faithful Holy Spirit always remained with me. He never deserted me, even in the middle of my messes!

I'd forgotten He was with me because I rarely talked with Him. I thought He was inside me to make me "feel happy" while a preacher was preaching "good" or a Gospel song was "winding me up" to feel happy. I didn't recognize God's Holy Spirit as the "God-Person" He is. I didn't know I could consult Him, anger Him, ignore Him, disrespect Him, silence and even grieve Him through the choices I made. For more than fifteen years, I had tried to make myself content with knowing I was a preacher's kid and that God had given me spiritual gifts and natural talents, but thinking like that only puffed up my pride even more. It did nothing to bring me peace or restore my fellowship with God—the Person.

Gradually, I noticed a subtle increase in my desire for more of God, though I was still holding on to a few ungodly relationships. As desire became thirst, I started listening to TV and radio preachers, searching for spiritual water to revive me. I preferred listening to one speaker who called sin what it is: SIN. He even named faults much like mine he had personally struggled against and overcome. One Sunday, he began a verse-by-verse teaching on facts *about the personhood* of the Holy Spirit. The more he taught, the more God revealed Himself to me and His truth revived my love for Him. In a flash, I recalled the time, location and occasion when I first received His Holy Spirit, filling me with joy and power, (along with the evidence of speaking in tongues)! I could hardly believe so many years had passed; I had forgotten the joy and sweet peace that filled my heart over the mystery of God's Spirit speaking (through my lips) languages I never learned!

After the broadcast, I turned off the TV and immediately slid down beside my bed, bowing low and humbly asking God, hesitantly, "Are you still inside me, Lord"? To my amazement, (I'm still holding back tears as I write), I heard the profound, but gentle voice of God's Holy Spirit say to me, distinctively and clearly, "I'm Here".

Hearing Him speak those two words FURTHER JERKED ME OUT of the sin I had become comfortable with, and changed my thinking! Suddenly I realized God had loved me enough to stay *with* me, in spite of my stubbornness and compromise! Now I *wanted* to be close to Him again and I *wanted* Him to lead me into discovering the richness of His warm "liquid love!" I *wanted* our relationship to grow and I *wanted* to love Him enough to stay with *Him*!

It is impossible to live a life of purpose in the Christ—life without the Holy Spirit's help from within. The Bible mentions our need for the infilling of God's Holy Spirit (for power to live for Him) AFTER we have believed and received Christ for salvation through repentance.

(Acts 19:2-7 NLT) states, *²"Did you receive the Holy Spirit when you believed? he asked them. (The King James Version and the New Messianic Version Bible* say "since you believed?") "No," they replied, "we haven't even heard that there is a Holy Spirit." ³"Then what baptism did you experience?" he asked. And they replied, "The baptism of John." ⁴Paul said, "John's baptism called for repentance from sin. But John himself told the people to believe in the one who would come later, meaning Jesus." ⁵As soon as they heard this, they were baptized in the name of the Lord Jesus. ⁶Then when Paul laid his hands on them, the Holy Spirit came on them, and they spoke in other tongues [a] and prophesied."

The Holy Spirit is the operational power of God whom Jesus sent to be IN and WITH His followers forever. Therefore, He instructed His disciples to wait for the *gift* of the Father (the Holy Spirit) *before* going into the world to preach and teach the Good News to everyone that God's kingdom has come to earth through Jesus. He told them they would *receive power* (to do the work He gave them to do) *after* the Holy Spirit had come on them. In essence, He was saying [in today's way of speaking]: *"Don't try to drive this new vehicle yet. The gas tank needs to be full of gas first, or you will not get very far without running out of power to move forward and finish what I commissioned you to do." [Pat's paraphrase].*

Power needs to fill every believer's human spirit before launching the Good News about Jesus Christ to those who are still living in ignorance of Him and His sacrificial love. Follow the example of First Century believers-in-Christ who, though full of passion and zeal, waited obediently to receive Jesus' promise of the Holy Spirit's power. Acts 2 (NLT) says, *¹"On the day of Pentecost [a] all the believers were meeting together in one place. ²Suddenly, there was a sound from heaven like the roaring of a mighty wind storm, and it filled the house where they were sitting. ³Then, what looked like flames or tongues of fire appeared and settled on each of them. ⁴And everyone present was filled with the Holy Spirit and began speaking in other languages, [b] as the Holy Spirit gave them this ability. ⁵At that time there were devout Jews from every nation living in Jerusalem. ⁶When they heard the loud noise, everyone came running, and they were bewildered to hear their own languages being* spoken by the believers. *⁷They were completely amazed! "How can this be?"* *they exclaimed. "These people are all from Galilee, ⁸and yet we hear them* *speaking in our own native languages! And we all hear these people speaking* *in our own languages about the wonderful things God has done! ¹²They stood* *there amazed and perplexed. "What can this mean?" they asked each other.* *¹⁴Then Peter stepped forward with the eleven other apostles and shouted to the* *crowd, "Listen carefully, all of you, fellow Jews and residents of Jerusalem!* *Make no mistake about this. ¹⁵These people are not drunk, as some of you are* *assuming. Nine o'clock in the morning is much too early for that. ¹⁶No, what* *you see was predicted long ago by the prophet Joel (see Joel 2:28-29). ¹⁷'In the* *last days,' God says, I will pour out my Spirit upon all people. Your sons and* *daughters will prophesy. Your young men will see visions and your old men will* *dream dreams. ¹⁸In those days, I will pour out my Spirit even on my servants—* *men and women alike—and they will prophesy. ¹⁹And I will cause wonders in* *the heavens above and signs on the earth below—blood and fire and clouds of* *smoke. ²⁰The sun will become dark, and the moon will turn blood red before* *that great and glorious day of the Lord arrives. ²¹But everyone who calls on the* *name of the Lord will be saved."*

The Holy Spirit is now in the earth, waiting to fill us and help us do God's will! No longer must we *wait* to receive Him. We just need to ask God to fill us with His gift; He's been longing for us to ask. The Gift is: "GOD *WITH* US, GOD REVEALED *IN* US"!

When we allow ourselves to receive, be filled with and be continuously led by the Holy Spirit as we read His living Word, He will lead us to do all Jesus foretold His followers they would do, namely "the greater works" (because He knew He was about to return to His Father). Jesus, Himself, promised *we* would do greater works than He did because He was going back (bodily) to the realm of the Spirit where His Father lives. Therefore, we must remain confident He did not leave us alone. He has sent His Holy Spirit to be with us and in us, empowering us forever to function as He functions!

This is not about you and me "feeling" spiritual. It's about *being* spiritual like Jesus, desiring, saying and doing what He said and did to show others the wonder and vastness of His Father's immeasurable love! It's about making His priorities our priorities. The Holy Spirit wants to empower more of us to reach many more people than Jesus physically reached with the Gospel! Billions more people populate the earth now than when Jesus lived here in the First Century. You do the math! He's waiting for you and me to become willing, and to become filled with His power—BEFORE WE GO!

My Place and Practice of Worship

As one of the five kids of a preacher, we met many preachers and pastors. Since then, I have seen some of the responsibilities of overseeing a "flock" of people, which involves m-u-c-h more than preaching or teaching from a pulpit. It's more than sitting in an office with a sign marked "Pastor" on the door. I didn't observe everything about those pastors from my youth because I didn't live with any of them day in and day out. However, I could gauge a little of their character and the quality of their love for God's flock by observing how they interacted with congregants.

I remember researching the habits and practices of Bedouin shepherds, and one thing stood out to me; it was how deeply they loved their flock. They made a habit of bedding down near their sheep, regardless of the smelly and uncomfortable surroundings. They always positioned themselves where they could know what was happening with their sheep. They wanted the advantage of responding quickly to their needs, day or night; because they knew sheep frighten easily.

During the day, the Bedouin shepherd was never far away. He or she stayed close enough to talk to the sheep, tend their wounds, soothe their hurts and make them rest, when needed. Shepherds both calmed and corrected their sheep, calling each one by its own personal name. Surprisingly, each sheep recognized its shepherd's voice, whether as one of authority or one of benevolent love. The Bedouin shepherd also knew how and when to administer tough (and tender) care, which she or he knew was the bedrock of a strong relationship with their flock.

In an amazing parallel, I discovered just how dearly God loved me, when I encountered His personal love through the unique care of a loving pastor He assigned to nurture me in my adult years. God chose this faithful under-shepherd to reshape my thinking through the power of His promises and commands. Later, He would choose others to guide the next phases of my spiritual growth, but this vigilant pastor spared no resource to mentor me spiritually and practically. To my surprise, I later discovered I was not unique. I was amazed at how this pastor invested heavily in every congregant's welfare! Such committed love caught and captured my attention, because I had never experienced it before.

True under-shepherds constantly remember God entrusts the lives of His precious sheep to their care as a solemn responsibility. The lives of the congregants *are* the "true riches" the Bible speaks of, and are far more costly than anything else. A true under-shepherd remembers the appointed day of reckoning, when God will ask for an accounting of how well he or she handled their responsibility to love and live godly before His people. His or her great sense of obligation to God keeps the true under-shepherd in a humble state of mind and posture of transparent service before God and people. In essence, they realize God has appointed and anointed them to uphold His loving standard with intelligence, patience, mercy and wisdom. Faithful under-shepherds choose to keep feeding their sheep with the revealed knowledge of God's word and a true, yet practical understanding (and interpretation) of His love.

God's Chosen Pasture

I began longing for more closeness with God when rhythm and blues songs failed to provide the peace and comfort I needed. No matter how talented the singer or musician I listened to, their songs left my emotions stirred, but my heart empty. Neither their words nor their voices ignited the spiritual fire of true joy for me. I was "shopping at the wrong store for the resource I needed" and my relationships with God and others remained strained until I could no longer "straddle the kingdom fence".

I wanted something much deeper and truly satisfying—something more! Hanging out with carnal friends and ungodly people only heaped up more guilt and shame, cluttering my conscience. No wonder my thirsty heart began to search for a way back to the spiritual peace I knew when I was young. (I just want to say, while I was estranged from God, Sunday mornings never felt quite right if I wasn't in church. At that time, I hadn't been in church on a regular basis for more than a decade)! My soul was so parched and hungry for regular spiritual nourishment, I was unaware my spiritual "tank" was close to empty. I thank God for His Word, consistently preached and sung on radio and TV. It was rich and consistent with Bible truth, and I could "feel" it filling me up like a satisfying meal.

Eventually, I began to realize no one feels complete in a vacuum; something else was missing. I finally discovered what I craved most was a sense of belonging and acceptance which only come through fellowship with other believers in Christ.

Sometimes, my mother would slip in a word of advice and say, "Patricia, take the children to church or at least Sunday school." I knew she was right so I didn't get angry at her reminders. (One thing we all loved about Mama, she never poked her nose into our business after we became adults, although she probably wanted to. When she did, she was always truthful and brief). Even my middle sister and her husband drove miles to urge me back into fellowship with God. They reminded me He wanted to be pleased with my service to Him. I knew they were right because my conscience was already preaching to me. (I didn't realize then that what I called "conscience" was really God's Spirit urging me, "Come back home and fellowship with Me.)" I knew in my "gut" I needed to join and regularly attend a good church teaching Bible truth, and I knew I should take my children with me. Still, I kept dragging my feet. (I remembered all five of us siblings not only going "to" church, but serving "in the business" of the church. Some of us sang on the children's choir, while others actively participated in some part of ministry.

Trying to live as non-Christians live convicted my conscience. I tired of feeling empty and outcast, so I took a first step and began sending my children to Sunday school on a church bus, which passed through my neighborhood every Sunday; I made sure they were on it. While my children were gone, I would think about how I could find a good church near us.

Since I was planning to go back to church anyway, I wanted to go to a "live" church, not one where if you said, "Hallelujah" when the preaching was good, people would turn around to see who dared respond "out loud". The TV and radio preaching had begun to stir up my spiritual appetite for "the real deal", not a "form" of godliness without any Holy Spirit power! I was looking for the kind of free expression of the Spirit I remembered.

A couple of weeks after the church bus started transporting my children I decided to drive them to Sunday School instead. It made more sense to drive them and stay, than come pick them up after only one hour. Besides, I loved the weekly teachings, as did my children.

Soon I decided I would also stay for morning services; this would be my litmus test. As much as I enjoyed the Sunday School teachings, the corporate worship did not meet my benchmarks. The sermon was heartfelt and accurate, but the moment I said, "Amen" in response to the truth, I saw heads turn, (yep, to see who had spoken out loudly in response to the pastor's message)! After those reactions, I decided to stay home on Sundays and enjoy God's Word via TV or radio.

At that time, my father was still Pastor of a mainline denominational church, and he believed everything he read in the Bible, even when his denomination's tenets disagreed. He practiced what the Scriptures (and Jesus) said believers should (and would) do, such as laying their hands on the sick for healing and church elders praying the "prayer of faith" over the sick. I was determined to do likewise, and through God's Word of Truth, He restored me to total recommitment to Him over time.

One day, I was engaging in "regular sister-talk" with my youngest sister when I abruptly asked her, "How can I find a good church—not a dead one, but a live one?" Her answer was, simply, "Ask God." Immediately, I asked her, "But how will I know when He answers me?" She simply said, "You'll know." So a few days later, I asked God, "Lord, which church should I go to?" When He responded, it was in His unique way and in His perfect time. Guess what, when that time came, I knew!

My Source of Supply

Growing up, I'm sure I heard sermons about giving, but I just don't remember much teaching about "tithing". I learned the tithe is first a way to honor God. When I tithe, I acknowledge Him as my Source of supply as I bring one-tenth of all my income into His storehouse, which is the local church or ministry feeding me spiritually.

I knew the word "tithe" meant "tenth", but I always wondered how the *practice* of tithing started.

I was well into adulthood before I learned tithing is an act of obedience demonstrating my trust for God's provision through the Law of Sowing and Reaping. Tithing is *not* about giving money, but all about putting God first above everything because His rightful place *is* "First Place". I learned tithing is part of a spiritual law of abundance, called The Law of Seedtime and Harvest. I could refer to it as, "The Law of Increase".

Through this immutable law, God teaches us how the kingdom of heaven operates. If you are a believer in Christ Jesus, the Kingdom of Heaven is *in* you (in your recreated spirit), and you (and I) must learn to live using more of heaven's resources. Everything that comes into the earth realm proceeds from the heavenly realm. It comes from God in seed form and increases, producing more seed to plant, more food to eat and more overflow to give away or invest in future productivity.

I've learned the more "seed" I sow (first to God), and the more I sow (plant) it from a willing heart, God increases my ability to keep giving to others who need it. (So, I become like a local branch of God's heavenly bank, a "storehouse").

I learned I can only give into the lives of others "as" my soul prospers. As my own mind, will and emotions mature in wisdom, God will speak through my spirit how, where and when to re-plant His abundance into good ground (areas with eternal value and productivity). This principle, I learned, is the key to prospering materially and growing spiritually.

God expects *all* His family to prosper and be in health, *as* our souls prosper! Hearing this excited me because it's so like God. My soul also prospers from learning and practicing God's laws of love. As I obey Him, I live under His protection where the curse on this earth cannot touch. It's called living under an "open heaven". Proverbs 26:2 TPT says, *"An undeserved curse will*

*be powerless to harm you. It may flutter over your life like a bird, but it will find
no place to land."*

So, I can do everything *God* says I can do, but only when my soul (my mind
and thoughts, my will, and my emotions) matures from following His written Word consistently.

Our Heavenly Father is beyond huge, beyond intelligent, beyond wealthy,
beyond anyone or anything we could dare imagine! When we acknowledge
Him in *all* our ways and in how *He* does things, we're saying, "Lord we
respect and love You highly!" As you and I pause to turn aside and devote
the first minutes of each morning to worshipping Him, (before we spend
time or money anywhere else), we're actually showing our Heavenly Father
we trust Him above all other sources of wisdom and supply! All supply lines
lead back to Him!

I had heard my parents discuss snippets about tithing, but I didn't know it
was a command. No wonder I always seemed to be scrounging to get enough
resources to pay my bills or provide better care for my children. I often
wondered why it was so hard for me (at first) to give to others, or to save as
I wanted to. God wanted to help me, but my resources were shriveling on
the vine due to a lack of knowledge about tithing! God could not "rebuke
the Devourer (the devil) for my sake" because I wasn't tithing. (Malachi
3:11) He couldn't "watch over His word to perform it" in my life, to the
degree He wanted to. His Word says to "prove" Him (by tithing) and watch
Him rebuke the Devourer, to prevent him from drying up our increase. It
was becoming clear why I never had much left over in those early days! By
ignoring God's commands, I was failing to bring the most important payment—the Tithe—into God's storehouse. Doing so would've proved God's
promise to pour me out a blessing so vast I wouldn't have had enough room
to receive it all.

The same Scripture, (Malachi 3:10-11), promises I will have plenty to give others in need if I plant seed. The tithe encompasses anything I offer to God first; it can be money, food, skills, knowledge, abilities, and even children—when I speak words dedicating them to God's service.

Although my wallet seemed to have had holes in it, back then, and my bank accounts seemed to have dried up sometimes, God instructed me how to break that poverty curse! He showed me how spending excessively and foolishly had become "a false god" to me. (Often, I had allowed a spirit of self-pity to convince me I should impulsively spend money I had set aside for important things. I was spending when I should have been tithing and saving). *I* was trying to make myself *feel* like I was as good as the rich, by storing up meaningless material trinkets. God told me softly, one day, "You are already as good as everyone else, because you are my beloved child."

Sister Wisdom

Regular chatting with my youngest sister was routine, because we felt like fraternal twins. We loved sharing praise reports, often touching briefly on the subjects of faith and tithing. I painfully remember telling her how it was hard for me to carve out enough money to give one-tenth of my gross income to God. I confessed I barely had enough money to pay my bills or buy healthy food for my children. (Often, I would settle for cheap cuts of meat and food of lesser quality, because it stretched my money's spending power). I didn't realize God wanted me to have the healthiest and best quality of everything. I was perishing for a lack of knowledge about my Heavenly Father's generous heart, and the vastness of my spiritual inheritance!

I will never forget my sister's advice when she said, simply, "Pat, you *can* tithe. All you have to do is pay God *first*, and you'll never lack or pay tithes late again." The profound, but simple, wisdom in what she said opened my ears to hear God speak through her words, and hearing it gave me the faith to believe I *actually could* tithe!

Suddenly, the whole concept of tithing seemed easy, the moment I "chose" to obey His wisdom, as my sister spoke it. By obeying her godly advice, I was choosing to honor God, the Source of all supply. So I thanked Him for entrusting me with the one hundred percent. Years later after maturing in my relationship with God, I thought, "I really can't 'give' God anything because everything is already His."

When I summed it up, "paying" tithes is similar to paying taxes, with one exception: The government *takes* the taxes I owe as a citizen *before* I receive my paycheck. God doesn't "take" anything from me or you because He wants us to *freely* pay it. He doesn't distrust His citizens of Heaven. He allows a hundred percent to come to us, including life, health, air, water, nature's beauty and bounty, and so much more! After all that, He sent His Holy Spirit into our lives when we asked Him. Then, as an act of our free will, He allows us to "choose" to obey His command out of hearts of love for Him. When I freely acknowledged Him with the first of my increase, He multiplied it by opening "Heaven's windows" and pouring all kinds of blessings into my life and into me! He does this so I will always have whatever I need in all situations and at all times, for every good work. Ultimately, obeying Him makes *me* a blessing to others!

I now know my ignorance of His Word means I am ignorant of His *will*, which prevents my flow of blessings from reaching me, and others. (Reread the Parable of the Talents that Jesus taught His disciples. He wanted them to "profit" in obedience *and* in substance. He wanted them to work with their hands, so they would have something to "give", not "lend" to others).

What a deal! He gives me a hundred percent, instructs me to use ten percent of it as seed to plant for a new harvest, then considers this seed a worship offering. He allows me to use the other ninety percent towards meeting the material needs in my life and others' lives. Every time I give to the poor, I lend to the Lord and He repays what I lent Him "with interest"!

Prior to that talk with my sister, I had struggled to keep our heads above water because I was not tithing at all. (I thought I was really giving sacrificially when, from time to time, I would decide to "squeeze out a whopping five-dollar offering" after I got my paycheck. I felt proud because five dollars was more than I had ever given in a single service. How precious was that)?

After I took my sister's advice, I could hardly wait for payday to come. It was easy to write my tithe check—first. It was as if God was smiling because I was in His will. I was honoring Him, willingly, and "showing Him" I trusted *Him* (not His gifts) to provide for me! Ever since then, God has opened Heaven's windows and repeatedly poured blessing after blessing into every area of my life. He stretches my faith to believe Him for His best because everything He gives (and does) is first quality! He enlarges my capacity to receive *and* my faith to give away more of my substance (time, clothes, money, opportunities and favor).

Fellowship with my Heavenly Father now grows more intimate as I thank and praise Him for showing His love for me! When I approach His Presence in prayer, worship or thanksgiving, I do so with the freedom that comes from knowing I have not robbed Him of the honor of receiving my tithes and offerings. I tithe because I love God and I love "how" He loves me. I love "how" He shows all of us He is our Provider!

The Takeaway: Choose to <u>not</u> worry. Remember, instead, what our Heavenly Father promised Noah after the Great Flood, "While the earth remains, Seedtime and harvest, Cold and heat, Winter and summer, And day and night Shall not cease." (Genesis 8:22 AMP)

Trust In God

Looking back, I've learned fear is a weapon the devil wields to bully God's children into indecision and confusion, and it thrives in environments of guilt, ignorance and unbelief. In this kind of heart-climate, fear fills a "faith vacuum" within us. It tries to distract us with lies, so we think our prayers of faith are not working. When this happens, we need to stop and ask, "Lord, what has blocked my prayers?"

I had to ask God exactly that question, when our gospel group finally finished recording, and was about to debut its second CD project, "Songs of Deliverance". We'd been frantically finishing all the details of our plan so we could hold our official CD Celebration, and had only one week to be ready. We'd secured a date and a venue. We'd planned what we would wear, the order of events, and printed the programs. The only action remaining—the most important—was the delivery of our hard-copy CDs and download cards.

That's when we received word our CDs might NOT arrive on time. After a few more days of waiting and praying, we finally accepted we would need to drive to New Jersey and get them. I volunteered to "ride shotgun" for another member of our group who said she would drive. Now we had a plan. Now everything was set...or so we thought.

Only forty-eight hours before our planned event, our volunteer driver informed us her job disapproved her request for leave. The moment I heard, I started praying harder, confessing God's Word and believing God would provide us another driver. In my heart, I was terrified I might end up the only one available to drive out-of-state (with only a GPS device to give me directions). It was my worst nightmare! I was more comfortable when I drove with at least one other person, especially when driving out of state. So I prayed harder, using every form of prayer I knew, but still couldn't seem to hear a clear direction from God regarding another driver. I desperately needed Him to come through quickly because the success of our event rested on having those CDs on time!

With only a few hours remaining, we still had no driver, so I decided to ask God why things weren't moving in accordance with what He promised in 1 John 5:14-15. The Passion Translation reads, *"And we are confident that he hears us whenever we ask for anything that pleases him. And since we know he hears us when we make our requests, we also know that he will give us what we ask for."*

I was combing my hair at my bathroom mirror, when I heard the voice of the Holy Spirit say softly and clearly, "If I regard iniquity in my heart, the Lord will not hear me." As soon as I heard that word from the Lord, my jaw dropped. Immediately, I knew exactly the situation to which He was referring, and I realized I was about to allow an un-confessed sin to sabotage God's plans for our group! Without God's help, I would never have realized I had an unresolved sin. (I knew God wanted me to confess something causing my conscience to feel guilt). Yes, He had heard my prayer for help with the CDs, but I couldn't see what was blocking the answer to my prayer until God's light of truth exposed it. Now I clearly saw the hindrance, as a flashlight suddenly lights a dark place.

When God said through the Psalmist, in Psalm 66:18, *"If I regard iniquity in my heart, the LORD will not hear me"*, He did not say, *"the LORD "did" not hear me"*. You see, God valued the integrity of His Word and our Father/ daughter fellowship as more important than even getting our CDs). He *wanted* to answer my prayer, but He wanted me to, first, get the wrinkles straightened out in our relationship, so they would not hinder my prayers. I knew if God were ever to violate His Word or alter what He previously spoke or promised, Heaven and Earth would pass away; that's what He said would happen if He failed to honor His Word. We know He cannot lie, so I knew immediately I must show the same integrity God showed when He reminded me of the truth in Psalm 66:18.

Quickly, I went into my bedroom and made a phone call. I urgently, and sincerely, confessed what I'd done, in disobedience, and received immediate, compassion and forgiveness from the person I called. As I hung up the phone, I now knew, confidently, God would help me get our CDs—*on time*. He had cleared the hindrance and answered my prayer. There was just one remaining challenge: I WOULD BE the ONLY DRIVER available! Now, I would REALLY need to trust God's Holy Spirit to guide me there and bring me home again! For me, this was BIG! Over 200 miles round trip, with only two days before the event, and all the miles were on major interstate routes during the evening rush hour. I felt like I was in a pressure cooker, with the temperature on "high"!

(Deep down, I think I suspected all along God was setting me up to trust Him in one of the areas He knew I feared most—fear of getting lost)! God was really doing me a favor by reducing my options. I thought, "I'm already in deep water; I can choose to swim or drown). I knew, now, I had to take off and swim like an Olympian, and I had to do it while I was still afraid.

My GPS and I gradually became good friends. Once or twice, it made some confusing changes but eventually, I made it to my destination. I must have circled my destination at least three times before finally figuring out how to get onto the property. My hands were sweaty and my back was tired from prolonged sitting, but I was pleased (and relieved) I had made it, with God's help. Later that evening I returned home, excited about pulling up to my door with our boxes of CDs, and a little smile of gratitude on my face. The overwhelming feeling of success made everything I'd gone through worth it!

Safely back at home, I asked myself, "What lessons did you learn, Pat?" I learned: (1) Through perseverance, I had not let the others down. (2) I overcame the spirit of fear by trusting the Holy Spirit's ability—not my own. (3) My heart had found a place of peace and rest in God, my Great Shepherd! (4) Accepting the Holy Spirit's confident leadership and tough love about prayer hindrances had made me more than a conqueror!

Wisdom Words: "Trust GOD from the bottom of your heart; don't try to figure out everything on your own. Listen for God's voice in everything you do, everywhere you go; he's the one who will keep you on track. Don't assume that you know it all. Run to God! Run from evil! Your body will glow with health, your very bones will vibrate with life!"

(Proverbs 3:5-8 MSG)

CHAPTER SIX

Choosing To Listen, Obey And Receive

More times than I can count, the Lord has proven He is Jehovah Jireh (My Provider) and Financier. He knows what's ahead and has already provided for all my needs. He grants the good desires of my heart as I pray, "Thy kingdom come. Thy will be done...."

Sometimes, God has not waited for me to ask Him to meet my needs, but He has timed my answer to arrive exactly at the time of my need. I think it's His way of reminding me He is All-Loving, All-Knowing and All-Sufficient.

Flashback

As I began to make slow, but steady economic progress, my budget was still tight, but as long as I stuck with it, it worked somehow. As the national inflation rate continued rising without my paycheck doing the same, we began to feel some economic strain. My children were growing older, as was their list of essentials. Sometimes, we barely got along, "robbing Peter to pay Paul", you might say. My bills had begun to slip into "slow-to-late status" and my credit rating, I won't reveal. Most of the time, scheduled maintenance on my car lagged until I could gather enough money to have the work done. That's how I learned the axiom, "slow vehicle maintenance is the same as NO vehicle maintenance". I killed two cars that way and I was growing weary.

One day while working, I was daydreaming about how great it would feel to pay my rent on time, just once. The more I thought about how delightful it would feel, the stronger my desire grew, until it dominated my thoughts. My monthly rent was somewhere in the low $300s back then, but it might as well have been in the low $3,000s.

I had already begun to "hold my breath", hoping I would have enough money for the payment by the approaching due date.

I quickly put the thought out of my mind and refocused on my work. After a little while, though, I sensed a gentle but precise "urge" to call my credit union, which was on the other side of the parking lot facing the building where I worked. Frankly, I could have walked the short distance. However, again, I shrugged off any thought of calling the Credit Union because I knew I had no money in my account. When your budget is as tight as mine was, trust me, you always know *to the penny*, what you have in the bank.

Again I returned my thoughts to work, until a stronger "nudge to call the Credit Union" interrupted me. This time it was so strong, it was like a "voice on the inside". The third time this "nudging" came with a firmer, but very gentle "whisper". (Frankly, I was becoming a little annoyed because it kept interrupting my concentration). Irritated, I said to myself, "O-kaaay, I'll call the Credit Union!" (I admit I didn't know why or to whom I was speaking with such impatience and annoyance). Then I mumbled, "Better still, I'll just get up and walk over there." By that time, I just wanted to silence the annoying, persistent urge.

As I walked over to the Credit Union, I could not believe I was en route to a place where I *knew* I'd sound foolish, as soon as they told me my balance was only the ten-dollar minimum to keep the account open. Right then, I *almost* turned around and walked back to my office, to my cubicle and to my work. Without knowing why, though, I kept walking toward the

Credit Union. When I stepped inside the door, I saw a long line of members waiting for service. As I recall, it was the day before a holiday and I was a little relieved to see so many people. Waiting for them would give me more time to "get up my nerve" to ask that ridiculously brave question, "My balance please?"

Finally, my time came to step toward the teller's window. She looked at me and smiled, and since I was slow to speak up, she asked me, "Would you like to know your balance?" Right then, R-E-A-L-L-Y softly, I cleared my throat and answered the teller, "Yes". She glanced at her computer screen, reached for a piece of notepaper and scribbled something on it before sliding it in my direction. I looked at what she'd written on the note and swallowed hard, but kept silent. Not sure how to respond, I slid the piece of paper back to her and asked falteringly, "Would you check that again, please?" (I was trying to sound confident, so no one would know how scared I was). The teller repeated her query exactly as she had done the first time, then slid the paper back toward me, again. Looking impatient and obviously wondering why I was taking so long to answer, she said (a little annoyed), "Miss, somebody up there must like you because the balance is the same as before. How much do you want to withdraw?"

The amount she'd written down was $738.00, but I was afraid to touch any of it because I was convinced it wasn't mine, and I know how fast banks recoup their money when they discover an error in their favor. So, speaking slightly above a whisper, I said timidly, "I'll take ten dollars," (just so I wouldn't look stupid). I also thought, "I can handle paying back ten dollars if it turns out to be a mistake in the Credit Union's accounting." Then I smiled faintly, took the ten dollars in cash and left the building (in shock)! I was overwhelmed! My mind was racing. How could I possibly have that kind of money in my account?

I waited until after the holiday, before returning to the Credit Union to check my account again. The money was still there, so I withdrew the amount of my rent, took it to my rental office and paid my rent—ON TIME! I even had a little money left over!

I still praise God, and thank His persistent Holy Spirit for amplifying the Lord's voice. Otherwise, I would have missed His provision!

Later, I learned that automatic payments on my recently paid-out car loan (financed by my Credit Union) had accumulated in my account. So yes, it was my money all along! (If I had known about the money, I probably would have spent it on something frivolous; back then, I had a bad habit of buying unimportant novelties to soothe my insecurity when depressed over a lack of money). Seven hundred thirty-eight dollars wasn't much by some people's standards, but it meant the world to me that day—the day my Heavenly Father proved to me He IS real, He DOES speak to me in my spirit and He really cares about *everything* that concerns me! He KNOWS everything—my strengths, weaknesses, likes, dislikes, good and bad habits— you name it. He knows me inside and out. You could say, "He knows me "all over, more than anywhere else"!

The Takeaway: "When you don't understand, trust God. When it's not in your hand, trust God. Don't know what to do? Trust God and He will open unseen doors for you." (Lyrics:

God of Miracles, Full of the Gospel, Songs of Deliverance CD, 2012)

Food from Heaven

Whenever I've asked God for help, He has always shown up with solutions to my needs; and I assure you there have been many—too numerous to count. I don't know why I always waited until the lack was pressing me before I'd pray. I think God even answered some of my heart's desires *before* I called to Him in desperate prayer!

The prophet Isaiah declared, *"It shall come to pass, that before they call, I will answer and while they are yet speaking, I will hear." (Isaiah 65:24 KJV)* Many times, the Lord has spoken a Word of wisdom to my heart comforting me with His peace; as a loving Heavenly Father, He already knew exactly what I needed and when I needed it, despite my hesitancy to ask. I believe the asking part is for my good. You see, before I ask I must force myself to believe and declare two things: (1) What I *think* I know and the little experience I *think* I've acquired can't meet the need I'm praying about. (2) I have a Father whom I know I can run to for help when things get scary, and He's ALWAYS been faithful to help me, no matter what!

Some of the times when I would *not* ask God to help me, pride had convinced me to think I could supply my own needs without God. My son still reminds me, "Ma, at the end of the day, we all need some help." Back then, whenever I decided "my way" or "my solution" was better than the wisdom found in God's Word, I was actually setting my own counsel above the wisdom of God. What a dangerous place I found that to be! Now I'm convinced God is my Father and He, alone, is responsible to provide for my needs.

A Word of Wisdom:

Just as I have comfort in knowing parents are responsible to provide for their children, so I realize I should've, first, asked my Heavenly Father to provide food for us. Instead, I always tried to convince myself we could "get by" until my payday. (Maybe God wanted to bless me differently than He had ever done it before).

One time when my refrigerator was nearly bare, I'd open its door from time to time and just stare into it, feeling helpless and hopeless. It seemed we were always running too low, too often, on too many necessities. I felt so depressed, sometimes, the extreme situation I saw would distract me from asking God for His help. Sometimes He could seem so far away when, really, He had never left me. I'm sure I was the one who did not have Him on *my* mind, as I should have. We had many needs back then, but this time our next meal was clearly at the front and center of my mind.

While talking with a coworker the next day, she asked me if I knew anyone who might want some beef. A little hesitant, I cautiously asked her how much it cost. She laughed, saying, "Oh, it's free!" I must have looked a little confused, so she explained, "Every six months my husband and I receive a shipment of dressed beef for our home freezer. Our next shipment will be here real soon and we need to make space for it. We're running out of time to clear out what's in there now, but didn't want to throw it away because it's still good, no freezer burn or anything like that." After she fully explained her circumstance, I could hardly believe when I heard myself say, "Sure, I'll take some of it off your hands!"

Sure enough, the next morning when I arrived at work, she was there waiting for me as she'd promised. I was shocked to see so much beef! Each piece was individually-wrapped for the freezer, and frozen solid, making it a lot easier to transfer to my trunk. I was also thankful I lived near my job, because we loaded so much beef into my trunk until there was barely enough room to close it! Both of us were delighted at what God had done without either of us knowing what He'd been up to!

God knew we both had a need. Neither one of us knew who He would use, or exactly how each of our needs would be met. We never dreamed He'd do it like this! At just the right time when we both needed a problem solved, He arranged for us to help each other! My coworker had admitted to me that the day before, she and her husband had no clue whom to ask about taking so much beef off their hands! They'd had a need and I'd had a need, and God connected us, so He could show Himself strong for each of us! He showed the kind of Father He is! (No one at my job had known I'd been using food stamps to supplement my income). I thanked God for the food stamps, but His heavenly solution far surpassed what my State could provide! Little did I know He wasn't finished providing....

God had changed our circumstances so my children and I were eating the best quality steaks and prime cuts of premium beef at NO expense to us! His abundant gift lasted many months. We had so much beef we didn't know what to do with it all! My grocery bill was m-u-c-h lower during that time because I didn't need to buy meat. This meant I had more money available to pay my bills—on time.

A few years later, my teenagers confessed, they had sometimes "incentivized" their friends to "visit" with them outside our front window when I was at work. (I did not allow them to leave the house when I was at work). So they would give each visitor a "gift package" of top-grade ground beef or a steak or pot roast to take back home. Their parents must have loved it, too, because we all lived in a government-subsidized housing community). The payoff for my son and daughter was double: (1) They were not violating home rules; and (2) they got to visit with their friends at home, though not *in* the home.

Takeaway: I KNOW the Lord will provide! He will make a way out of no way, even when we fail to humble ourselves and ask for His help. "He" becomes our way of escape so we can bear up under any adverse situation.

CHAPTER SEVEN

Choosing To Receive Genuine Love

Hospitality

I was still reserved and introverted when I first arrived at the small church in the county where God led me, although I tried to mask it. One of the divorced mothers reached out, inviting me to have lunch at her home during my lunch break from work. She lived a few miles from my job, so I accepted, feeling pleased someone in the fellowship had noticed me. I usually preferred keeping a low profile in new situations, but this invitation was different.

Her home was impressive, and after greeting me, she then led me to her dining room, where my jaw almost dropped in surprise! She had set her table with beautiful china and crystal stemware. It was exquisite, like it had been set for a meal with someone prominent. She'd planned the meal thoughtfully and prepared it beautifully! The food was light fare and satisfying, without weighing me down after my return to work.

I'll always remember this friend's genuine hospitality, even as we chatted pleasantly and appropriately. Neither of us really knew each other well, but her warm welcome transmitted God's love and acceptance at once. I felt as if God had seared my heart with His love-brand, where all could read, "I love this little daughter of mine!" Who else, but God, could lead me to a midday banquet displaying a welcome like this! I sensed this would begin a close friendship between us, and it has lasted throughout the decades.

A few months after our special lunch, I became a member of the church, although I already knew from the moment I stepped over the church's threshold, it was "home" for me.

Not too long after that midday lunch, this young mother called me again, but this time she sounded hesitant and a little apologetic. After chatting a few minutes, she was about to end the conversation, but suddenly changed her mind and shared a financial need she was hoping I could help with. I invited her to my home to explain the situation further, and she came.

After explaining her situation, she asked if I could lend her the money she needed to pay her car note on time. I was willing to lend her the money, but I confessed I did not have that kind of money on hand. (I, too, was a divorced mom on a shoestring budget). Then she explained she would only need the loan for a few days until her payday, at which time she would reimburse me. I really wanted to help, but I needed the money for my own car payment.

I really felt "a pull" to help her, though still unsure how I would decide. I thought, "Do I help a friend in need, or do I look out for my own needs first? Finally, I chose to take the risk and told her I would lend her the money. I added the stipulation that I must have it back in time to pay my own car note, coming due in just a few days. She was grateful, reassuring me that she would return the money on the same day she received her paycheck, and we hugged to seal our agreement. I was pleased to help, and she was happy I could. Then I walked her to my front door and began my good-byes. The moment I began closing the door, I heard the voice of God's Holy Spirit say distinctly, "Now I want you to trust *Me* to repay the money, not her." I felt a settled peace as I heard Him say those words in my spirit, although I wasn't exactly sure what it really meant. I just knew I should obey His direction.

Sure enough, when my friend's payday arrived, she called me, but I could hear her disappointment. She told me the paychecks had not yet arrived, and sadly confessed she didn't know what to say to me because she knew a promise was a promise. I felt sorry for her predicament because she seemed "stuck" with no way out.

I wasn't sure what I would do either, so I began checking around for sources I could "tap" to find enough money for my car payment. I checked each of my bank accounts, finding a little money in one, and then a bit more in others until, finally, I had the amount I needed. I don't mind telling you I was shocked, but oh, so relieved! I never realized I had extra money in those old accounts! Ecstatic, I withdrew the money and paid my car note, ON TIME!

The next day, my friend called to say her paycheck had just arrived, and she wanted to bring the money to me right away! What a relief we both felt. Hanging up the phone, I breathed a sigh of relief and remembered the Word of the Lord and the instruction His Holy Spirit had whispered to my heart as I'd closed my front door a few days before.

Tearfully and worshipfully, I remembered God knows everything in advance of it happening. He knew those paychecks would be late. He also knew my friend's situation was a great opportunity for me to use my faith as I learned how to trust Him to meet my needs, while He used me to help with the needs of another!

He already knew I had some money, and He knew where it was! How grateful I was for His protection and Fatherly care! I felt stronger because I'd trusted God and used my faith in Him to help a friend who had befriended me. The bonus: I still had the money she repaid; I had a new sisterly friendship and a far deeper relationship with my Heavenly Father. He was helping me build new relationships. How sweet was that?

Wisdom Word: "A friend loves at all times, and a brother is born to help in time of need." (Proverbs 17:17 AMP)

Intercession

Prayer Warriors in Spiritual Warfare

I never knew the importance of heartfelt prayer until God chose a select group of prayer warriors to rendezvous at my new home church about six months after I joined. They were among a group of military service members (and their families), who had changed duty stations from Germany about the same time. The duty station for most of them was at a nearby military installation. Most of them were friends, but from different branches of the Armed Forces. They all seemed to know the secret to serious and powerful prayer, both in the Spirit and in their intellect! I had never seen people pray with the kind of explosive power I witnessed in them. When they prayed, I saw situations change for the better! Most of my experience had been in the area of studying and teaching, but I did not have the discipline for serious, prolonged prayer, as they all did.

I watched and listened intently to everything they did and said, because I was learning. I observed their habits—how they lived, studied, repented, and fasted to keep their consciences free of known sin—and free from anything that would hinder God's answer to their prayers. I hung out with them every chance I got, attending intercessory prayer conferences and other events with them, whenever possible.

They all (male and female) were serious prayer-warriors. Maybe their deep commitment to prayer resulted from their orderly and disciplined military lifestyle. Whatever the reason, I wanted to learn how to recognize God's voice, as they did. Continuing in their company, I learned more about God's ways, and more about the Biblical way to fast, worship, pray and praise. Wow, did we have fun learning how to flow with God's Holy Spirit!

One of the female soldiers in the group blended into my family right away, and eventually became godmother to most of my grandchildren, nieces and nephews. She was a no-nonsense Christian, and committed to living godly. Her integrity was unimpeachable! Many of my extended family members admired her because she lived what she believed, with no shortcuts. They especially admired her unselfish investments of time, talent, treasure and prayer. As I watched her example, I learned the importance of integrity, loyalty, friendship, confidentiality, covering our Pastor in prayer, and especially the value of waiting for God's timing. Her way of living mentored across generations—from me to my daughter, then to my daughter's children. (Even as toddlers, some of my nieces and nephews would pretend to lead praise and worship service, sing and beat the tambourine as she did). The power of the gospel she lived spread even to my son's life, inspiring him to embrace his role as a minister of the Gospel of the Lord Jesus Christ, even while he faced life issues as a teen, a young adult and a young father.

It seemed inevitable we would become prayer partners, and she was definitely a prayer mentor. When I married for the second time, she was my matron of honor. A decade later, she made sure my oldest granddaughter (her first goddaughter in my family) attended intercessory prayer conferences and other prayer events to learn what other prayer warriors could teach her about the benefits and power of prayer. She took time to invest in my granddaughter's spiritual life after the night she observed her actually speaking in the Spirit (tongues) before she could walk! More than a few times, we noticed her, barely able to stand, but holding onto the sidebar of her crib, buckling at the knees in time to music and speaking clearly in a language my prayer partner, my daughter (her mom) and I confirmed were "tongues".

It was amazing! In our hearts, we knew she would be a dancer and an intercessory prayer warrior. Today, her life has revealed the fulfillment of both offices—and more, as have the lives of my other grandchildren and family members.

From this supernatural connection, God showed me praying for others is a privilege I get to share with our Heavenly High Priest (Jesus Christ). In Heaven, His redeeming blood constantly cries mercy for us here on earth.

As I matured in the things of God, I sensed He knew when I needed just the right laborer, seasoned enough in spiritual things to understand my ignorance of praying in the Spirit, and mature enough to overlook my faults, (pride being among them). God gave her the grace to show me how to eat wisely, so my body could withstand a rigorous life of prayer. Then He gave her the grace to model the discipline and sacrifice required of a good soldier of God.

I watched this laborer's life closely, and one of her habits even taught me how she avoided arguments.

I'll never forget the day she began to share exciting information she had learned from a preacher we both respected. As she shared some of the details, I began to express "my opinions and objections". I noticed she quickly became quiet, which shut down the conversation. I knew in my spirit her actions were saying, "When someone rebuts what you're sharing, it means they probably disagree, and two people cannot walk together (much less talk together) if they are in disagreement." She chose silence, to keep me from continuing in critical conversation, which could have ended with me criticizing God's anointed preacher (and God), without realizing it. Since then, I try to use the same rule to govern how I respond to new information.

The Holy Spirit also used her to tutor me in listening for (and recognizing) how God can answer prayers. I'll never forget the time she said, "Pat, the more you pray softly in tongues under your breath (even during preaching and teaching), the more you will sharpen your ability to hear the Holy Spirit when He speaks to your heart concerning the things He wants you to know or do."

Many times, when we prayed (in spiritual warfare) for others, we were amazed at God's faithfulness! One time, we were interceding for my daughter's husband; he had suffered life-threatening injuries in a serious motorcycle accident. We prayed in agreement and in the Spirit for many hours before we heard the doctors say, "We almost lost him to cardiac arrest twice, but we finally succeeded in bringing him around again!"

During one of our Thursday night intercessory prayer sessions, when she and I were the only attendees that night, we were praying in tongues for people in authority, and neither of us could remember the name of a former dictator of the Philippines God wanted us to pray about. We prayed hard and long in the Spirit, and as I closed my eyes to block out all distractions, I suddenly "saw" the printed name of the dictator coming toward me out of the darkness. At first, the words were very small, but the more we prayed, the larger they became until I could read them. At that very moment, I shouted out the words, "FERDINAND MARCOS"! We rejoiced over the Holy Spirit praying through us, because He knows everything!

My prayer partner was accurate about so many things, so I finally surrendered my pride saying, "Lord, help me to respect this woman of God as a person who hears Your voice, by experience. Teach me what You have taught her, because I want to hear You clearly, as she does."

He answered my prayers, as she introduced me to Hebrew terms, Hebrew textbooks, the meanings of Hebrew and Greek biblical words, and to some of the writings of the sages, until I built a substantial Biblical library of references, and other resources. God was calling me deeper into the school of the Holy Spirit; and I'm thankful I followed Him.

Waiting to Inhale

Twenty-four years later, I had walked in faith with my intercessory prayer partner through trials, hardships and triumphs, until early one very foggy February morning my phone rang. She only said, "Pat...." As soon as I heard her faint voice on the other end of the phone, I interrupted her, saying, "I'll be right over." (As I'd left her house the evening before, the Holy Spirit had prompted me I would be back there very soon). I thought it would be to sit with her during the night, so she would have someone to talk with). You see, for close to twelve years, while praying for others, she had fought hard through a series of health attacks and I, among others, had been helping with some of her housework the day before.

On the morning she called I wanted to rush, but the Holy Spirit told me to take my time and drive safely, because of the heavy fog. As soon as I stepped inside her door and closed it behind me, she said, "Pray." I did my best to pray as I had seen her pray for so many others. Then, in the middle of my prayer, she asked me to help her stand up. While I was lifting her from her chair, the voice of my prayer partner and friend fell silent. Wondering why she didn't answer a question I asked her, I repositioned myself to look directly into her face and, that quickly, I could see she had left her earthly body and crossed over to be with Jesus in her spirit body. I just stood there in quiet awe, still waiting for her to inhale....

I remembered her telling me, "Pat, each time I've prayed about my situation, the answer I always got from the Holy Spirit was, 'Wait.' I know He would never have told me to wait, if He wasn't coming." That morning, He kept His promise.

As I contemplate how God has taught me, I clearly see that He teaches us best through relationship—with Him and with others. Oh, I could have read about intercessory prayer in books, which I did many times in those twenty-four years, but I learned more as God taught me to study people. As He taught me how to intercede, I also learned other things I had no clue I needed to know.

I was like the rich young ruler who thought he had figured it all out, and checked off everything on his "bucket list" of tasks to inherit eternal life. However, God knows everything we need to know, have and do in order to live a successful, purposeful life in His will. I have learned: "Relationship" is the environment where we learn best to do His will, IF we will decide to "milk the moments".

CHAPTER EIGHT

Choosing To Believe God

For Health

When we were young, Mama suffered from attacks of recurring chest pain, caused by arrhythmia (a condition in which the heart beats with an irregular or abnormal rhythm). Whenever this happened, she'd stay in bed awhile. After Daddy received his call from God to preach, Mama would send one of us downstairs to get him so he could pray for her heart. He'd stop whatever he was doing to come place his hands on her head, and pray. The five of us would perch in the hallway, just outside the threshold of their bedroom door and watch. Sometimes the arrhythmia was so severe we could see the bed moving because of the irregular vibrations of her heart!

Soon after Daddy placed his hands on her and prayed, we would watch as the bed slowly stopped shaking. No sooner than it had stopped, Mama would smile and tell him her pain and discomfort had stopped. Afterward, she'd get up, get dressed, and go back to whatever she had been doing.

This was my earliest introduction to Jehovah Rapha, (though, back then, I didn't know this redemptive name of God). He was the same God who also spoke to Moses in the Wilderness of Shur, when the people needed deliverance from disease because they had complained against God's provision. There He made a statute and an ordinance for them which included the promise, *"...For I Am the LORD who heals you." (Exodus 15:26b NLT)*

When my mother had asked Daddy to pray a healing prayer, the Lord responded in the "present tense", showing her, "I *Am* the Lord who heals [keeps healing] you."

Years later, as I looked to God for a fellowship of believers to join, God's Holy Spirit used this childhood event as a benchmark for identifying the place where He wanted me to serve Him. So when I visited the little church He led me to, I felt right at home when, to my delight, I discovered they believed in preaching the unadulterated Truth of God concerning divine healing. They believed Jesus, the Living Word, still heals today through faith in His Word of Promise, just as He'd healed in Biblical times.

The more I listened to the preached Word and studied it, my heart would leap with joy and anticipation at God's revelation of His Son—our Healer! Up to that time, I'd never experienced supernatural healing personally, but I remembered I'd seen it each time Daddy had prayed and laid his hands on Mama's head. I had seen her recover and resume her normal routine the same hour! I remember thinking, "Now this is the kind of God I want to serve! I don't want to serve "a god" (little "g") which is too impotent to heal!" I wanted to serve the God of miracles (the God of the Bible)!

I began soaking up the preached Word and studying my notes for confirmation, then practicing what His instruction said, not just for healing, but for other needs, too! I could hardly wait for each service! Each service, I was in my seat—waiting; every time, on time!

I had only attended the church a short time before the devil tried to steal my new growing faith for supernatural healing. I didn't yet know the Scripture about how Satan comes *immediately* to steal the Word of God I'd heard and received with joy. Mark 4:1-20 is about a parable Jesus told, after which He explained its meaning to His disciples. It reads,

"And these are they by the wayside, where the word is sown; but when they have heard, Satan [the adversary] comes immediately, and takes away the word that was sown in their hearts." Mark 4:15 NMV (New Messianic Version Bible)

Little did I know I was about to enter a "spiritual fight" to hold onto the truth of supernatural healing God had confirmed in my heart. I thank God, now, for my father's obedience to act on the Word he had studied and believed, concerning God's credibility and reputation as a Healer! The picture of his obedience stays in my mind.

My Test

One beautiful Saturday afternoon, my teenage children and I were leaving my middle sister's home, when the chilly wind of a spiritual storm began to stir. Still chatting, we got into our car to leave; my son was driving and my daughter sat in the rear seat. (My son was still gaining driving experience, so I sat in the front passenger seat). I will always remember the sky that day—a beautiful soft blue—and the trees were thick with dark green leaves. A soft, gentle breeze punctuated the end of a perfect day—but not for long!

Fastening my seatbelt, I remember feeling a sudden twinge of low-level pain just under my rib cage on the left side. I dismissed it, because it felt like the pain that happens when I run too hard; but then I thought, "I haven't been running." Soon I noticed each time I breathed deeply, I felt that little twinge of pain. Again, I thought, "Maybe it'll go away once I take some slow, deep breaths." However, the pain remained. Before our car had left their driveway, the pain and discomfort had worsened, and I began thinking this might be more serious than I thought.

Suddenly, I "saw" myself in a casket! I saw and heard no one speaking, yet I "understood the vision" loud and clear, AND its message. It was a threat from Satan (a lie he wanted me to believe). The hair on my forearms stood at attention as I sensed something evil near me. Then, surprised, I heard myself "answer" the threat, saying boldly from my spirit, "It's either you or me, devil, and it's NOT gonna be me!" Though I spoke no audible words, I knew immediately in my spirit the battle had begun!

As soon as I answered that challenge with my heart's voice, I heard the clear voice of my Shepherd (God's Holy Spirit) calmly instructing me, "It [the pain you're feeling] is Pneumonia". Then He quickly said, "But don't speak it aloud." He alerted me it was a lie the devil was trying to get me to accept. He let me know Satan was trying to steal the fruit of my faith (the Word I'd recently heard and believed—the truth that God still heals today). Then God's Holy Spirit began tutoring me. He told me details I needed to know and things to do and say, to build up my faith. He wanted me to remain unshaken as I walked through this valley of the "shadow" of death.

The closer we came to home, the pain intensified. After reaching home, only a thirty-minute drive, I could barely breathe without feeling the stabbing, searing pain. (By the way, my son and daughter had no clue about the battle raging in my mind because all of my fighting, up to that point, was in the unseen, inaudible realm).

The pain soon grew worse! Each time I tried to breathe deeply, the pain felt like it was stabbing my lung. It seemed to be saying, "Oh, no you don't! I'll tell you how deeply you can breathe because I'm in control!" So I only took shallow "snatches" of breath each time I inhaled. In my heart, I knew I must fight this battle of faith with only the Lord as my "Counselor" and my "Rear Guard", and He boosted my faith for what was to come!

Three days later, my breathing was still shallow as I faced a crossroads. I had to choose, whether to go to work on Monday or call and request sick leave. (Before I go any further, I want to caution every reader: God's methods of delivering His children are so vast and unique, they are past finding out, meaning we can't assume we know *how or what method*

He will choose to deliver us). What I mean is this: He's not limited to using methods He might have used in the past, even as He had healed my mom or anyone else! He is Creator God and He knows all the things we need healed or changed in our lives. He also knows how to fix every situation, and the right people to use, not just those *we think* are perfect to soothe our distresses. Your health may not be restored in the same way mine was, so don't make the mistake of trying to "rubber stamp" another person's healing experience. Just follow the leading and the instructions of the Holy Spirit within you, and He will "walk you through" each trial uniquely! He will put the right people in place and show you the right steps to take.

Meanwhile, I wrestled with the decision to call and request excusal from work, due to illness. My problem was I didn't want to say I was sick because I thought, "Wait a minute, sick people call out sick, but I am the healed of God; I am His child, and there is NO sickness in Him". So, I went to work, in spite of the painful, shallow breathing!

The next few days were days of instruction, even amid the mental and physical battle I was fighting. The less able to breathe I became, the more fear tried to subvert my thoughts saying, "You're gonna die!" I even tried visiting family to help refocus my attention away from the intensity of my mental and physical struggle. I didn't know, then, I should've been focusing on what God's Word promises. I noticed fear diminishing whenever I focused on something "other than" the incessant, searing pain. Then, it would worsen and I could hardly breathe at all. So I called my pastor for more advice about how to "stand in faith" until the health Jesus gave me through His shed blood fully restored my body.

After hanging up the phone, I immediately began doing what I'd just been counseled to do. As I sat on my bed with arms encircling my knees, and rocking back and forth, I said (in spite of shallow breathing), "Thank You, Lord, for my healing." I did this repeatedly, offering it as my prayer of petition and declaration of thanksgiving. However, after I'd thanked God this way (out loud) two or three times, I distinctly heard the Holy Spirit's gentle voice of Truth calmly "correcting" my confession. He said, "Don't thank Me for your healing; thank Me for your health." Immediately, I understood He was correcting my lack of knowledge about the redeeming work of His Son at Calvary! You see, *in Christ* I am already whole; "I" am NOT sick, though my body may suffer attack! In fact, I am "the healed" person the devil is trying to "make sick" He knew he could give me sickness, only if I *gave him* my God-given authority by choosing to accept his lie. What an immediate relief I felt! That revelation of truth instantly reinforced my faith, in spite of the pain! Hearing God's personal instruction brought joy into my struggle, and His joy strengthened me to keep fighting!

The devil's next strategic attack came as another "death threat". Despite the pain, I was sitting on my bed reading my Bible, still barely able to breathe. Suddenly, an intruding thought invaded my mind saying, "If you don't go and see a doctor, you're gonna die!" When I heard it, I thought, "So, what's the worst thing to happen if I die?" When I asked myself the question, I "saw myself" (mentally) getting into a small canoe-type boat, peacefully pushing away from the bank to cross over toward the beautiful shores of Heaven. Immediately, I said aloud, "Oh, so I'll go home to be with God—so what? Why should I fear that?" Immediately, the threatening voice fell silent and I knew I could stay in the fight. (However, lurking in a corner of my mind was a nagging little temptation to consider getting medical attention). Then, I heard a faint echo of unbelief say: "If I'm not better in two days, I'll go see a doctor". (It was the unbelieving voice of "Plan B").

The next day back at work—still taking shallow, painful breaths—I had a thought: "I should get my Bible out of my desk drawer and read it." Confidently I whispered, "Oh, You want me to "take in" Your Word like I would "take" prescription medication—every four or eight hours—like that?" The moment I heard the still and gentle voice of God's instruction, my joy and peace increased. I knew I was in safe hands because God's Holy Spirit was guiding and guarding me all the way through this!

Opening my Bible to read, I remember wondering, "Which passage should I read?" When I didn't hear any immediate answer (like a sure knowledge, seemingly coming from nowhere), I just flipped to a page and began reading. As it turned out, I was reading from the New Testament Book of I John, Chapter 5, verses 14 and 15, NKJV. The passage was new to me, *"14 Now this is the confidence that we have in Him, that if we ask anything according to His will, He hears us. 15 And if we know that He hears us, whatever we ask, we know that we have the petitions that we have asked of Him."*

The moment I read verse 15, a powerful thing happened! I really have no earthly words to describe it, except when I read the words "we know" that we "have" the petitions..., I felt a profound "inner explosion of power" in my chest, and the direction of its force was moving outward (from the inside)! The impact of God's revealed truth (His "rhema") hit my spirit and my chest so forcefully, my upper body "buckled backward a little" from the impact! It was as though the force of a mini bazooka had exploded inside me!

Hidden within God's written Word, the "logos", had been God's rhema! The "ammunition" (truth) He instantaneously showed me was in the form of a "Word of Knowledge". That Word was *"ALREADY"*! When my eyes read His promise, "...we know that we *have* [*present tense*]...," my life changed forever! The God of All Comfort—my Healer—had transferred "Zoe" life (which is life as God has it *right now*) from His Holy Spirit to my body, and the Truth of *"already healed"* became flesh in my lungs! I personally felt His glory in my *own* lungs, and the glory was full of Grace and Truth! *I knew I was healed—ALREADY!* In spite of the pain, God's Word had completely chased away the LIE my feelings had been trying to get me to believe! The truth was exactly as the Holy Spirit had whispered a few days earlier as I'd sat on my bed and heard Him say, "You are 'the healed' because you are My child, and the devil is trying to 'deceive you' into accepting sickness—*because* you are My child, and he hates you."

When I grabbed hold of this truth, I felt exactly as I do when I visit my doctor, and he writes me a prescription for a powerful antibiotic or antihistamine—then hands it to me, and says, "Take as directed!" I don't know about you, but when a doctor hands me a prescription to remedy whatever's ailing me, I feel immediately peaceful and relieved because I know it's a done deal! Even as I swallow my first dose, still feeling every symptom of sickness I'm battling, I'm still confident it's *only a matter of time* before they diminish and disappear! So, although the pain, infection, and inflammation blocking my breathing were still there, I *knew* in my "knower" it was only a matter of time before they, too, would disappear!

Wow, did I rejoice! I could hardly contain my praise and thanksgiving! (I had to remind myself I was still at my desk; because I really wanted to climb on top of it and SCREAM MY THANKS for the restoration of my lungs)!

God had rewarded my "little faith" to trust Him as my Divine Physician, and His promise (His Word) was the written prescription! I had accepted the desire *He* placed in my heart to trust "Him" and let "Him" restore my health. Sure, I could have "chosen" to have a human doctor prescribe medicine to treat my symptoms and relieve my discomfort, but I would have missed an opportunity to grow in intimate fellowship with God, my Healer as I was learning to know His ways. I, also, would have missed the privilege of receiving the customized, loving instruction He, alone, can administer (one-on-one). No matter what we need, He wants to guide all His children, because He dearly loves and cares for us.

Epilogue to This Experience: For many years, I thought I had stood the test of endurance to receive my healing that day, but as I wrote about how it happened, I realized I actually had received a MIRACLE from God! You see, healings are gradual and can take time, but miracles are instantaneous! Just as Jesus answered the rich young ruler's heart-question when asked how he could inherit eternal life, God had been teaching me a deeper lesson: I must learn to be patient as I wait for Him to mature my faith in Him. Patience is a *fruit* of the Spirit. Meekness is another *fruit* of the Spirit, defined as "humility" and "strength under control". God was not only restoring health to my body, He was giving me a practical exercise in "being" teachable to first prosper my soul (See III John 2).

When He saw my childlike faith to endure the waiting period was beginning to weaken (as I considered seeing a doctor if my breathing didn't improve), He "expedited" the answer to my petition by sending it to me via "spiritual express"! It was the same petition I asked for (and believed I had received) when I prayed! (I John 5:15)!

All along, He knew exactly where my levels of faith, patience and meekness were, because my relationship with His Word had been weak.

So as any loving parent watches closely when their child takes his or her first few steps of faith and begins to walk, they move closer to that child to encourage them to keep standing, my Heavenly Father had sent an angel to "swiftly meet me" at my personal level of faith! Now, my faith is stronger to stand through future skirmishes, which will surely come.

God was confirming that His All-Powerful reputation never tarnishes! When He makes us a promise, He keeps His promise *every time*. He is the same yesterday, today and forever! His name means: "I AM" (NOW); I Will BE WHO I WILL BE *because* I AM. PERIOD. Jehovah Rapha means I AM the God that "healeth" thee. The "eth" means I healed in the past (though it was still your present); I AM still healing in the present (TODAY), and I will continue HEALING in what you call the future; but I AM

ALWAYS in the NOW! I live in the ETERNAL NOW! So ask of Me, because I AM WHATEVER YOU NEED!

Wisdom Word: I let the doubters, the scoffers, the fearful and the unbelieving say whatever religious-sounding rhetoric they choose to say, because I now KNOW the God of the Bible—the God of Abraham, Isaac and Jacob—is the only Healer, the only Great Physician and the only true Lover of my soul. I know this because I am His child! He personally cares for me and for all of my needs, even when I get in His way. For this, I am eternally thankful and unashamed to acknowledge our love relationship to the world!

For Promotion-Flashback

"This I know: the favor that brings promotion and power doesn't come from anywhere on earth, for no one exalts a person but God, the true judge of all. He alone determines where favor rests. He anoints one for greatness and brings another down to his knees."

Psalms 75:6-7 (TPT)

As I was learning to wait for God to promote me at work, I did not know He had already seen ahead and provided for me. I now realize "good things come to those who wait—on *God's* plan and timing." Growing up, I'd heard some older people say, "I know the Lord will provide." I had heard gospel songs declare it and I recalled the phrase often when I began working full time.

I started small in the work world, like most people. My first job after graduating high school was as a Coding Clerk, when computer use was in its early days of implementation. When my small family moved out of state, I worked as a File Clerk with a different federal agency. Within the same year though, I had returned to my home state where I worked as a Long-Distance Telephone Operator. Although I enjoyed chatting with customers, the job just didn't pay enough for me to run a household, and its leave policy didn't work well for me. I later moved on to fill a Telephone Operator vacancy at a local federal agency.   A major federal hiring freeze was in progress, but God gave me favor and they offered me the job! Later I accepted a job on the midnight shift with a different office. After a couple of years there, I started chasing promotions. To supplement my anemic income, I even worked some part time jobs along with my full-time one.

Eventually I had to stop working multiple jobs. Too often I'd found myself driving while asleep (with my eyes open)! The final "sleep-driving" incident shocked me into moving closer to work. A year or two later, I finally got a slightly better position on the same Federal installation, where the benefits package was better than what my previous jobs offered. I was most thankful the new job helped me get *off* the roles of my state Welfare system, where I'd been stuck for too long.

As my son and daughter grew older, I knew I could no longer afford to be away from home in the evenings. So I quit working part time to be home as they grew through their turbulent teens. Exhausted one day, I overheard myself whispering a sigh, "Lord, what I *really* need is a promotion on my day job." Soon, I began applying for Federal internship vacancies, which were developmental positions, combining training, work and study to pre-pare the intern for successive non-competitive promotions over a two- or three-year period. When I applied, I was pleased my academic degree gar-nered one or two extra points for me in the rating and ranking process.

When I finally learned I was among the top three contenders, I also heard rumors about shady practices by some employees in the recruiting office, so I doubted if I would be the one they selected. When I finally heard I was "not selected", discouragement drove me to apply for intern vacancies *out-side* my preferred field. One intern vacancy occurred in the Education Office on the same federal installation, but it only reached a target grade *two* levels above my current grade. The first intern position I'd applied for had a promotional target grade *three* levels above my current grade. Of course, I preferred that opportunity.

Soon, I overheard coworkers whispering I should file an official Equal Employment Opportunity (EEO) Complaint to investigate whether I was a victim of job discrimination. I had never heard of the EEO complaint process, but as I began thinking more about it, I finally decided to file a complaint. (I was about to learn just how frustrating the bureaucratic "waiting-and-response-process" could be)!

To summarize, I was "not selected" for the first intern vacancy in my office. It went to someone who could barely speak or write English. Soon afterward, my office filled a second, and eventually a third intern vacancy. Those positions were also in my office, under the same open announcement for which I had originally applied. I couldn't figure out why I had not been selected for one of the other two vacancies, because my name had been at the top of the "Best Qualified" list since the first announcement opened.

For two long years, I waited for the "federal bureaucratic machinery" to grind through its tedious processes. Each day I reported to work, laboring to look unaffected by what had happened to me. I struggled to be a positive professional, but inside, I grieved.

One day, I was feeling pressure from the added stress of responding to letters of negative preliminary rulings from the EEO Office, and it was getting to me. As I pushed through the day, I felt a surge of negative thoughts and emotions overtake my defenses in a silent second! I couldn't hold back my tears another minute. Self-pity and disappointment were attacking all at once, and I remember thinking while blotting tears away, "This is just not fair!" I was considering just giving up on this rigged bureaucratic process! God, however, sent many people to help me stay in the game. Some of them strengthened my resolve; others encouraged me; still others refreshed and even prayed for me as I waited those two stressful years. One person volunteered to be my legal representative, *at no cost to me!*

Of course, I accepted the offer! Another person (a friend) even looked me straight in the eyes and said, "You are going to see this through to the end. You are *not* going to quit!" Their grave tone of voice had the force of a command, and it must have chased away my feelings of doubt because on the spot I felt a "rush" of resolve well up in me. Instantly, I knew I could (and would) pay the price to stay in the fight!

After all the court battles, negative rulings, praying, crying, doubting and asking forgiveness for doubting, I finally got some news. My youngest sister, who worked nearby, stopped me as she returned from lunch one day and said, "Pat, as I was driving along the road just now on my way back from lunch, I had an "open vision". *(An open vision is a sudden flash of insight into an event while awake—not daydreaming or sleeping).* She continued, "As I was turning the corner into the parking lot, I suddenly saw what looked like a giant court file or folder with lots of papers in it, and your name was typed on its edge. On the cover of the folder was stamped in large bold letters, the word: 'V-I-C-T-O-R-Y'!" She looked me in the eye and said, "God said, 'You've already won!'"

My heart leaped as I felt tears of disbelief stinging the corners of my eyes. It just sounded too good to be true! I was almost afraid to believe it because my case had received adverse preliminary rulings at every juncture of the two-year process! I wanted desperately to believe her report and believed what she'd seen was true. So (by faith) I carefully said, "Glory to God, I receive that!"

The next day, my supervisor pulled me aside to tell me my case had indeed been resolved and the court had ruled in my favor! My supervisor said I would receive instant credit for the two non-competitive promotions I would have had in those two years. In one day, I had jumped two pay grades A-N-D I received the "back pay" for the two late promotions! To top things off, my final non-competitive promotion to the third pay grade happened soon afterward. My supervisor announced, "Effective immediately, move all your personal belongings from the desk where you sit now, to the new desk where you will receive intern training! I praised God for bringing me through!

More Change

I could hardly believe after waiting and wondering for two long years, my "due season" was rushing in and overtaking me! So many changes in one day overwhelmed me! It goes without saying I was "awed" at God's timing! He had been my Faithful Advocate in the court process. He had fought (and won) all my battles without requiring one penny of my money. He had given me favor with key people when I needed it most, and He had won a decisive victory for me in the face of all forms of opposition. God had guided me strategically through every hindrance. He had matured me with timely wisdom and had taught me self-control by His Spirit! I am still living in His provision and mercy!

However, God had not finished with His plan to mature me. His goal was (and still is) to refine me to look, act, and function in maturity, like Christ. He was moving, shaking and shifting situations to continue molding me into His instrument of gracious change. His purpose has been to influence my life and the lives of every person I encounter. By His Spirit He kept teaching me how to forgive and release grudges. He has shown me how to handle challenges (and even threats) with grace. He still teaches me to respect authority to improve faulty systems, while respecting people whose cultures, appearance, opinions, values and politics may differ from my own. I spent five years working, growing, and changing, to incorporate the knowledge and wisdom I gained while in the trenches with God; I discovered I *could* change, but only if I were willing to take the incremental steps moving me toward *God's best*.

During later assignments, I learned to adjust to sudden changes brought on by work related crises. (Sometimes, I pushed against change because I was uncertain about doing something I'd never done before). I finally concluded, "There really is no healthy way to avoid changing!" I watched the dynamics of our Division change drastically when roles and relationships shifted as managers changed. The dynamic voice of change shouted to us all, "Deal with me and make it work!"

Within two years, I began rotating as Acting Division Chief. Suddenly, the only remaining senior specialist in my office decided to retire. The timing couldn't have been worse for me! Several important year-end reports were due and I knew there was no way I could produce them on time. I struggled to coordinate all the required sections of the report, but most of my coworkers were engaged in learning new duties, which slowed our progress.

Only a year before, I had been the only "junior specialist", comfortable submitting "only my portion" of the report. I hadn't needed to concern myself with its final submission because it was the "Division Chief's responsibility". This year, I had become both the only senior specialist AND the Acting Division Chief within a thirty-day period! I don't mind saying I was afraid that I would fail!

Now the year-end report was due and my Division was among only a few others needing to request more time to prepare a response. I was frantic! I had just barely rallied enough courage to apply formally for the permanent position in which I was now acting as Chief. Now, fears attacked my confidence: (1) How could I even dream of getting the permanent position if I were late submitting our most important report; (2) What kind of impression would a poor response make in the mind of the selecting official; (3) How in the world would I handle this fiasco? Reluctantly, I phoned my supervisor (who was now the selecting official for the vacancy I was temporarily filling) and requested a meeting.

In the meeting, I explained the changes happening with our staff and its impact on our group efficiency. I explained how the recent changes could slow the gathering of our data, and what I would need to meet the deadline. Finally, I summoned all my courage and carefully said, "I will need an extension of a few days beyond the due date to be ready with our portion of the report." Then I waited politely for a reply. (I knew as I stood there, this "glitch" was happening at the wrong time and I could feel the fear in my heart escalate). I feared others might regard me as incompetent, especially for the promotion for which I had now applied. I also feared "losing face" and the opportunity for this important promotion.

My supervisor's answer, when it came, amazed me! Quietly, I was told my request for more time was granted! However, the reason it was granted, both surprised and humbled me.

You see, in my heart I knew I had not *earned* this kind of mercy! This mercy came because my supervisor said she had great respect for someone who was willing to admit a problem, but still request what was needed to research, complete and submit an accurate report! I knew it had to be God, working in my supervisor's heart (and on my behalf), because He is the God of Mercy AND the God of another chance!

Again, He had made a way of escape for me! Those next few days gave my staff and me the time to compile accurate information and meet our extended deadline! My "God of Another Chance" had now revealed Himself as my Deliverer!

God was calling me to cleanse my "self-righteous heart" (because I thought I could "earn" a promotion). Only the Righteousness of Christ Jesus was sufficient to make me promotable!

The Message Paraphrase of I Corinthians 1:30 says, *"Take a good look friends, at who you were when you got called into this life. I don't see many of "the brightest and the best" among you, not many influential, not many from high-society families. Isn't it obvious that God deliberately chose men and women that the culture overlooks and exploits and abuses; chose these "nobodies" to expose the hollow pretensions of the "somebodies"? That makes it quite clear that none of you can get by with blowing your own horn before God. Everything that we have—right thinking and right living, a clean slate and a fresh start—comes from God by way of Jesus Christ. That's why we have the saying, 'If you're going to blow a horn, blow a trumpet for God.'"*

So the voice of my trumpet heralds this triumphant proclamation: The God of Abraham, Isaac and Jacob, the Only God, the God of Heaven and Earth, and the God of Heaven's Armies has done great things for me by the strength of His Mighty Arm and according to His unique plan for my life! He has taught me to wait on His wisdom, His timing and His deliverance for the sake of His greater plan!

Take Away: "The Lord is good to those who wait for Him, to the soul who seeks Him.

(Lamentations 3:25)

Peace and Rest

Choosing to believe my heavenly Father's counsel over the threatening voices of trouble and turmoil became my personal practice. Each challenge forced me to dig into deeper levels of faith in God's promises. Confident in His desire *and* ability to heal my body, I began to "coast" on that experience. The Bible encourages me to be anxious for nothing, but in everything by prayer and supplication, with thanksgiving, I should let God know what I needed, and I was learning to do that.

As I became comfortable with knowing God as my covenant Healer and Provider, I decided I should become more diligent in guarding my part of the covenant (the details of my life I control). I started scheduling routine checkups for my sight, hearing, and general medical health. This included scheduling my first mammogram. I wasn't too thrilled, but I knew it was necessary.

At the doctor's office, I felt "butterflies" in my stomach. I reminded myself I had nothing to fear because God had promised to be with me through everything life could throw at me. After the first images, the technician told me, "I'll be right back; I have to get the doctor to read your film." I waited for what seemed like a long time before she returned. When she returned, she said the doctor wanted me to stay a little longer, so they could perform a sonogram to see the image better. A little anxious, I braced myself because I did not like the direction of the conversation.

After what seemed a lot longer than before, she returned to tell me the doctor wanted to schedule a biopsy, because he saw something suspicious he wanted to check out. Suddenly, my mind reeled with all kinds of wild thoughts. (One of my worst fears had been the fear of having to endure a mastectomy. I remember conversations years ago with my Mom, as she described her experiences with women who'd had the surgery. Since then, I always said I didn't know what I would do if I ever experienced a mastectomy). I know, now, the devil had listened too. He was hoping I would allow myself to doubt God's promises and provision. *My* mistake was thinking God would heal me the same way He had before.

On my way home, I thought about my faith position, that is, where (and on what Scripture reference) I should anchor my faith in God's deliverance for this situation. I asked myself, "Pat, what do you *really* want to happen?" That was easy for me to answer: I wanted them to perform the sonogram and, Voila! The sonogram would be clear! I did not want *any* kind of surgery to mar my body with a scar.

When I showed up for the sonogram, it was a lot like my mammogram experience, and the report came back the same. (I couldn't understand why my faith hadn't worked.) Remember, I wanted to see "nothing" on the sonogram! When I returned to my Primary Care Doctor, we talked and he asked me what I wanted to do. I said, "I want to wait a little longer to see what happens." He seemed a little annoyed during our discussion. (I suspect he didn't see a reason to wait before scheduling the biopsy). I wanted to wait because I wanted God to make the image disappear *before* the biopsy; I didn't want a scar for the rest of my life. I'm not sure if my reason was vain or not, but I was trying to activate my faith to get exactly what I was believing God for).

Well, "I caved" in my decision to hold out, because I didn't want to displease my doctor. After all, he was a kind, pleasant sort of person and when I saw his irritation with what he thought was hesitation on my part, I didn't want him to think negatively of me. In short, I didn't have the nerve to stand my ground and say what God said about my health! That ole "fear of man" spirit was still whispering in my ear, just like when I was a child "trying to fit in" at home; I pretended to understand my doctor's reasoning and agreed to the biopsy, which he scheduled right away.

On the day of the procedure, I remember being "prepped" for anesthesia. As they started, I remember feeling a deep, settled peace about "going to sleep", and I remember saying, "Holy Spirit, I trust You. I know I'm safe in Your arms. So, I'll just relax and close my eyes, and when I awake again, I will still be with You, and I won't remember anything of the procedure." What I'd spoken is exactly the way it happened! I remember waking up, with no recollection of the procedure. Then, I heard the news I was waiting for. The doctor said, "The tissue we collected and examined was benign." "There is no cancer!"

I was relieved to hear the report, but later I thought, "Pat, if you hadn't let fear railroad you into believing the lie it dangled at you, you would have gotten *exactly what you were believing God for,* which was *no* scar to mar your body *and* a good report! "There never was any cancer in my body! I chose to believe a lie that caused me to fear.

Lesson Learned: I *already had* the petition I had desired from God, when I prayed! (I John 5:15). God wanted me to see it was *my* choice to remain steadfast and unmovable. I only had to "stick to my guns and back up my play" with rejoicing, praising, rereading His promises and *not* changing my decision, even for my nice doctor! However, God's compassionate Holy Spirit reminded me I *did* win. I *did* enter into His rest as I went under the anesthesia. He reminded me to *resist* the message of guilt the enemy wanted me to feel because I didn't hold out till the end. He reminded me that we grow "from faith to faith".

Now, I hardly notice the scar; it has almost disappeared. Yet, a remnant of it remains as a "marker" of when I dared to believe God and I chose to rest in His comforting arms, regardless of the outcome! I bear the marker, reminding me that during times of fear and unbelief, I must always trust God's Word until the end! My adversary is still defeated!

"Put on the full armor of God, so that you can take your stand against the devil's schemes. For our struggle is not against flesh and blood, but against the rulers, against the authorities, against the spiritual forces of evil in the heavenly realms. Therefore, put on the full armor of God, so that when the day of evil

comes, you may be able to stand your ground, and after you have done every-thing, to stand." (Ephesians 6:11-13 NIV)

For Comfort

I've experienced God's delivering power many times. As I recall, each deliverance was different, and I suspect will continue to be different from any preceding it. The timing of each deliverance was both unexpected and surprising! Sometimes, God's ways of escape were private, and at other times, dramatic! *He* chooses to demonstrate the power of His comforting love in seclusion *and* openness. He has proved He alone was my Promoter or Burden Bearer, which still astounds me! Regardless of "the how" or "the when", His supernatural deliverances have always been profound and unique!

Try as I might, I've never been able to imagine "how" God would answer my prayers or cries for help! I finally concluded it was best if I just keep enjoying both His spontaneity *and* provision. Besides, I think He enjoys surprising me with His "wow factors" and His "unique signature" on every miracle He performs. Often I say of my relationship with Him, "It's not so much *what* He does (because He's always faithful), but it's *how* He does it."

Flashback

No one is ever prepared to receive news of a loved one's passing. As a child I would try to imagine how I'd feel about such things every now and then—how it would feel, perhaps, if one of my parents passed away. Sometimes, those imaginations tried surfacing in the form of a nightmare, but waking up brought instant relief. On the other hand, after I became an adult, things changed.

A few months before I retired from federal service, I actually experienced hearing that shocking news! On a gorgeous October evening, after I had returned home from work, I was so exhausted I fell asleep fully dressed! I'd planned to relax only a few minutes, since I didn't feel sleepy, but I remember waking up a little later, surprised to discover the sun had almost set, and somewhere in the stillness of that beautiful Indian Summer evening I could hear a gentle, but persistent knock at our front door.

As it turned out, my husband answered the door and told me my younger sister was waiting in the living room to talk to me. I thought it a little odd that he announced her visit, since she lived only blocks away and it was normal for us to pop in and out of each other's homes for informal visits.

So I moved from the bed and nestled into a chair; as I heard her faint footsteps approach. At first, she paused in the doorway with her hand still on the doorknob. Then she stepped inside the room, and I remember her gently saying, "I didn't want to call, so I decided to walk down here to tell you Daddy went home to be with the Lord at eight o'clock this evening. Apparently, he had a massive heart attack."

Well, the strangest thing happened when I heard what she said. From my heart surged feelings that were then, and still are, hard for me to explain. They were feelings of celebration, triumph, and even accomplishment! Where were these emotions coming from, which enveloped and overwhelmed me?

In a flash, I'd seen a clear mental picture of Daddy victoriously crossing the finish line of a race well run! I didn't deny my sister's news was true, but I felt so proud of this finishing accomplishment, I could barely suppress my excitement.

He was the patriarch of our family, and he'd been the first to cross the finish line of his race! He seemed to be setting a benchmark for the rest of us—an example for us to follow, so to speak. I was even more amazed because I felt absolutely NO grief at all—NONE! I even *tried* to feel sad, but in vain. Somehow, I knew intrinsically God's Holy Spirit was shielding me by giving me a quick glimpse into Daddy's finish-line experience! I felt so full of joy I wanted to shout the victorious news through the roof that my Dad had finally made it over the finish line! (By the way, I did not share my feelings with my sister).

After she left, I just sat there with a crazy half-smile on my face, reminiscing about the times when Daddy would analyze our singing rehearsals, saying, "First, stop and get your harmony". He'd sometimes jokingly say, "I don't want to be looking over the banisters of Heaven watching y'all trying to sing, if you haven't first stopped to get your harmony right." It all seemed surreal as I sat there, awed that the day he had talked about so long ago and so many times had finally come!

Days went by and I expected to "come down to earth" about the reality of what had happened, but the uplifting joy remained. I felt like I was in some sort of cocoon. Grief simply could not get near me, much less attach itself to me! I tried, but I simply couldn't find any reason to grieve or be sad. (I know each of us reacted differently to the reality of his passing, but for me *nothing* was loss—everything was all gain)! I knew my heavenly Father had me in a protected place shielding me from feelings of hurt and loss. I was safe in His secret place—the place the psalmist described in Psalm 91. I felt like God had tucked me under the shadow of His huge cozy wing where I could hear His heart beating the cadence of Daddy's victorious graduation march. Under His protective wing, I felt secure. I never imagined it was possible to be so shielded by Heaven's reality that grief, or any other negative thing, could not penetrate!

For three months, I never cried or even wanted to cry. (I am confident God knew what I needed). He knew the truth of His Word and the strength of His new covenant with me could (*and would*) withstand anything this life could throw at me! He wanted me to know it, and He showed it.

A few months later driving home from work, I was trapped in bumper-to-bumper traffic, which had grinded to a halt. I decided to make my "down time" productive by phone-paying one of my bills during the wait. As I scrolled through my phone contacts to find the creditor's number, I happened to scroll past contacts listed under "D". Suddenly, my eyes were looking directly at the entry "Dad" and his home phone number. *Suddenly* I realized I would *never* again talk to Daddy at that phone number, and I was surprised to feel my tear ducts quietly filling up, responding to the fact that I was going to miss my Daddy's presence here in the earth.

Later, when I asked God why I hadn't grieved over Daddy's passing, he responded gently, and profoundly, "You couldn't feel grief because you were *never fatherless. I* have always been your Father and I always will be." (Isn't that just like God)? I'm so glad my earthly Dad introduced me to God, my "real" Father, early in my life. He has proved His faithfulness in demonstrating He alone is, and will always be, my God of All Comfort! I could try to say more, but there is really nothing else left to say. God said it all!

"And the peace of God, which surpasses all understanding will guard your hearts and minds through Christ Jesus." Philippians 4:7 (NKJV)

The Takeaway: "All praises belong to the God and Father of our Lord Jesus Christ. For he is the Father of tender mercy and the God of endless comfort. He always comes alongside us to comfort us in every suffering so that we can come alongside those who are in any painful trial. We can bring them this same comfort that God has poured out upon us."

(II Corinthians 1:3-4 TPT)

CHAPTER NINE

Choosing To Change My Focus

Challenging My Limitations

Sometimes change doesn't happen when we expect it, or "as" we expected. We can never quite be sure if we're up for any task, even a task we want to achieve with all our heart unless we, at least, step into it! Facing threats and challenges from a posture of fear is something every human tackles on the journey from birth to death. (I told you about how fear harassed me during my young life, trying to convince me tragedy would overtake me. The threat stopped for a short time, but later returned intermittently, threatening me until I learned to fight back by resisting its solicitations. Even so, we all must stand ready to do battle with the threat of fear because it will continue to attack.

"Fear of Failure"

While, obviously, I continued to live beyond ten years old (as the lying deceiver repeatedly threatened I would not), he then tried using another approach to limit progress in my God-assignments. Many times, I'd become excited and accept a new assignment, but the moment I did, a lying spirit would attack my mind and the spirit of fear would say, "You can't do that" or "You don't know how" or "You're going to fail!"

In my singing assignments, threats would assault my mind saying, "You can't reach that note" or "Your voice is going to crack as soon as you reach the end of your range!" As much as I loved singing, I would shrink back from accepting ad lib or solo parts, because I didn't think I could handle them. (Those to whom God has assigned ministries requiring the use of a vocal gift are frequently challenged in the same way).

Flashback: At our Junior Choir rehearsal, the Choir Director assigned me the lead part for a song we were learning. I was so excited I went home and practiced it repeatedly. However, every time I approached the section, "Everyday, I pray Lord...," I would back away from the highest note, afraid my voice would crack when I sang it. In my discouragement, the Choir Director kept encouraging me, saying, "Go for the note, Pat. I know you can sing it!" I had believed the lie that I just couldn't, so I left rehearsals feeling guilty like I'd let everybody down.

A couple of days passed, and I was at home lying across my bed thinking about the song's lyrics. The song began with the request, "Lord, keep me day by day, in a pure and perfect way; I want to live on in a building not made by hand." Oh, how I wanted to sing the improvisation exactly like Eddie Williams, who sang the lead part, with the "The Caravans" (gospel group) in the background. Every time Eddie sang it, I'd feel my heart warm with God's Presence, and I was moved to tears of joy! However, each time I approached the ad lib, my courage shrank, because I believed my voice would crack.

Then I thought, "If I could just find a place where I could practice it real loud and nobody would hear it, then I'd feel free enough to 'go for it' at the rehearsal". Just at that moment, I had a strong "thought"; (I had not learned to recognize the Holy Spirit's voice back then because I was only twelve years old). However, I was sure I felt (or heard) a voice directing me to look beside me, where I noticed a throw pillow, and the voice said, "Pick it up and cover your face with it, to muffle the volume as you sing out loud." As I did exactly that, wouldn't you know it; the fear and the lie immediately went mute, and I sang the phrase LOUD AND STRONG, *just as Eddie Williams sang it*! (My voice never cracked)!

My confidence soared! Not only did I reach the highest note, I realized the top of my range was even farther, once fear had released my throat! Fear had constricted my vocal cords in the past, and the lie had suffocated my courage. From then until now whenever I sing, I know to simply relax and let God's Spirit DO what Satan suggests I cannot do! That's how I challenge barriers threatening to restrict my song!

Changing My Song

God gave each of us gifts from His great and varied supply of spiritual gifts. He intended us to use them well, as we serve one another in brotherly love. God has also charged parents with the responsibility to guard their children and guide their use of the gifts and talents He has given them. Spiritual gifts are to serve *God's* purposes, accomplishing good and imparting life. The devil has no ability to give good gifts or create anything, yet he constantly tries to lure us into traps to misuse our powerful talents and gifts. Perverting the use of God-given gifts wound others and detour us from fulfilling God's plan for our lives. Our adversary can only steal from us and *try* to kill us *if* we fail in our vigilance. He plans to destroy our families and godly reputations, but only IF we allow it by failing to study his strategies.

In his jealous rage and pride, he seeks to destroy the blessings God meant us to richly enjoy and share. He also takes advantage of our lack of knowledge about God's loving nature. If we unknowingly leave open opportunities our adversary can exploit, he will derail our progress to paralyze our godly influence.

"Get Your Harmony"

As I mentioned earlier, I can still hear Daddy saying that to us. He frequently reminded us of this because we sang without musical accompaniment. He would ask, "How can three people start singing in three-part harmony, if they don't first determine the key they're singing in? If they don't establish the right key for the song, how can their harmony blend?

When we were first learning to sing (as young children), we were selective about our harmony and our sound. I could even say we were a little picky and prideful. All our young lives we hoped someone in the mainstream music industry would "discover" us. As it turned out, that was not God's plan for the song He placed in our hearts. He did not want us to "commercialize" or "compromise" our message or our musical sound, and nothing we tried to do really "took off" as we had hoped. Though some are, we were not called to do that.

We were devastated at first, even pouting a little. I do admit I was a little jealous of other groups whose music seemed to have "made it" to where we aspired to be. (Sometimes, I was even snobbish about our musical ability (just my opinion), although I tried my best to appear humble. At times, we were a little "puffed up", but I guess some of that pride is the nature of immaturity. Growing up, we were sometimes a little cryptic toward other family members who had good singing voices and tried to join in as we sang. We really loved singing without musical instruments, preferring instead to clap or play tambourine as we sang.

We did become frustrated over the years when we could never seem to find a pianist able to devote time to playing exclusively for us. (Maybe that was also part of God's plan).

We sang at weddings, funerals, reunions, you name it. One time a local promoter "ripped us off" after we ministered in song and invested money in special outfits. When the event ended He told us, "I couldn't fill the venue, so I didn't collect enough money to pay you." In my opinion, that incident sadly reflects the worldly idea of "singing for a living", and it's all one big scam. The last time I looked, mainstream music production has not changed (because of the love of money). As young people, we had no business acumen, pursuing "the world of the song".

In that world, the rule of law is "Survival of the Shrewdest and Greediest". This is just my opinion, and I've never found anything in Scripture *even remotely* sanctioning so-called "Gospel Competition". The term is an oxymoron. It is a prominent example of how the satanic agenda has corrupted church music by inserting the devil's warped agenda to incite jealousy.

After years of struggling, unsuccessfully, to commercialize our music brand, we began to develop a growing love relationship with the Word of God and the God "of" the Word. That's when we discovered God's *true song* is *in* His Word. His Son *is* the Living Word, so when we spent time reading and meditating Scripture, His Holy Spirit downloaded the songs of Heaven into our spirits.

He fashioned all of us and put His gifts into our hearts and minds. *He* wanted us to use those gifts to impart life, joy, strength, restoration and encouragement to people who would need rescuing from the ditches and cesspools into which their life-choices had thrown them! God wanted us to know singing was never about "making" music *or* money. It has always been about lingering in God's presence until He serenades us with His heavenly song so powerfully that we have to write it down and sing out *His* song through our lips!

(Of course, we were all grown up with families by the time we finally understood all this. God stayed with us, though, faithfully teaching us more about Himself and the riches of His grace and mercy)!

By far, I've enjoyed singing gospel music, because its joy explodes and becomes vitally contagious, flooding me with peace! God's music produces love, joy, worship and victory! When we were young, we sang in church and local choirs all around our city, and sometimes out-of-state, just because we loved to sing God's music. Years later, we discovered we needed to know more of God's Word before we could accurately model His character and sing of His goodness with power. Eventually I observed the more we lived god-like, the more powerfully His presence rested on our songs. Though I knew Christ as Savior, I had a lot to learn about maturing in His patience and living with integrity under His Lordship.

<u>Another Flashback Moment</u>: "Sorry, They Will Only Sing Gospel"

To this day, I thank God for a Dad and Mom who actually prayed "against" our so-called "success in the mainstream music industry". They didn't tell us until many years into adulthood that they'd prayed, "God protect our girls from the devil's destructive plans to pervert their lives and their songs." They did not want to see us caught in the downward spiral of singing spiritually dead songs for fast money or fame, or both. They never wanted us to live low lives that pushed us closer toward calamity!

I suspect Satan has always been jealous of the musical gifts God's children now have. They formerly were his exclusive gifts, until pride was found in his heart and he was ousted from heaven! So now, he tries to ensnare every musician and psalmist with the corrupted fruit of pride, arrogance, jealousy, competition, which produce corrupted living. These pollutants rob our songs of their power to heal and deliver oppressed people. Ministry through song is far more than a "catchy tune or cadence".

As we began singing with a few renowned artists and traveling to sing in other states, our parents' prayers protected us from many potential mishaps and derailments.

"Songwriting"

I think the creative expression we've enjoyed most has been songwriting and dramatic presentation. Songs, hymns and spiritual songs still pour effortlessly from our recreated spirits into our hearts, minds and mouths! When they do, we still feel compelled to write them down because we regard them as God's gift to (and for) everyone.

We were thrilled when we finally connected with a first-rate recording studio and produced some of God's inspired songs for the common good. The "in-studio experience" intrigued us as we learned to appreciate the technical knowledge of (and collaboration with) studio technicians and instrumentalists. We learned to place music production in a class by itself!

The devil's "wild seed of desire for fame and fortune" has taken many years (and mistakes) to purge from me what was sown in foolishness. God, however, has remained faithful. He delivered me from the warped condition of "religion without relationship" as I experienced the God of the Song "re-igniting" my heart's song. Through His song, He restored my soundness of mind when my will dissolved. When the stress and pressure of hard times threatened to compress me, or empty religious activity proved powerless to lift the burdens I carried, God always breathed songs of deliverance into my heart and my mouth, stirring my joy and increasing my strength. He still speaks to me using song lyrics and stanzas!

Sadly, many who chased the wrong song discovered, too late, that it only leads to a dead-end. As a naïve gospel singer, I invested far too much time and money trying to fit into the world's "rigged" system, instead of seeking God's counsel to find out what *He* wanted, which was miracle healing music. God still blesses me with opportunities to sing His praises every minute of every day of my life!

Wisdom Nuggets

(1) Keep trusting that Father always knows what's best for each of His children. (2) He uses our experiences to refine and develop us in our service of love to others. (3) Jesus created His music *in* us, making it easier to enter the holy atmosphere of His presence, which transforms our lives.

(I believe God answered our parents' prayers. They had seen the wisdom of Proverbs 14:12 play out in the lives of too many other singers, great and small. It reads, *"There is a path before each person that seems right, but it ends in death."* I'm glad God helped me keep *His song* in my heart! He yearns to hear coming from my heart, the rich treasure He deposited there).

One of my favorite things to do is harmonize with background singers, when the harmony is what we musicians call "tight", and anointed psalmists play their instruments as God leads. In that environment, the Lord's presence increases until miracles happen, and God's love becomes visible and tangible! As His presence intensifies, everyone becomes one in perfect unity and harmony! This is when we begin to "know" Him in a unique way, unique to each of us, but common to all of us who belong to Him, because *He* is the God of the Song!

Stranger in My Bedroom

I've heard some say faith is like a muscle; you've got to work it to keep it strong. I agree, because there have been times that made me challenge what I *thought* I believed. You see, I've been living the faith life for many years now, and I thought I was pretty strong in the "faith department". I had learned many scripture references about faith, even rehearsing them daily.

I've learned fear is the opposite of faith and F-E-A-R means "False Evidence Appearing Real." I can quote the Scripture found in Philippians 4:13 reminding me I can do all things through Christ, which strengthens me. I also heartily agree that greater is He that is in me than he that is in the world! I've been confessing and agreeing with these and other faith building Bible verses for more than thirty years. However recently, my thirty-year-old "faith" underwent a test.

One evening while I watched TV and snuggled under thick cozy covers, something briefly distracted me. When I glanced away from the TV to check it out, I saw nothing so I returned to watching my program. A few minutes later, I thought I saw movement again, to my right. Again, when I glanced in that direction, I saw nothing out of the ordinary. Then I thought, "Maybe it's something in my eye or maybe a speck of dust on my eyelash." Rubbing my eyes, I went back to watching my program once more.

All of a sudden, I saw a black shadowy image dart across the ceiling! Reflexes made me sit up and reach quickly for my blanket, which I swung in the direction of the moving shadow! This time I thought, "Oh my God, there must be a bird in my room! I was mortified with fear, so I threw the covers over my head and tried to tuck every corner of the blanket around me!

Then I got *real* quiet, straining to determine if I could still hear the "flapping of wings". I heard nothing—dead silence. After a few sweaty minutes under the hot covers, I eased my head out a little and peeped to see if the coast was clear. I felt queasy and horrified as I wondered, "How in the world did a bird get inside my house—at night!"

All of a sudden, the fluttering began again, and the fluttering sound was coming closer! Finally, my heart couldn't take any more shock, so I stood up on my bed and began to swing my covers around and around my head toward the ceiling, hardly believing what I saw: there was A BAT IN MY BEDROOM!

Right then, I felt my skin really begin to crawl, because in my mind's eye were the haunting scenes of every *Dracula* movie and *Dark Shadows* episode I ever watched! I wanted to scream and cry and run—all at once; but where was I going to run? The only other family members at home were fast asleep! Repeatedly, I called loudly to wake them but after a while, I was convinced even "The Rapture" wouldn't wake them! So I did another "belly whop" onto the mattress, quickly diving under the blankets one more time, and there I lay, real still and tucked-in. I wanted to be sure the invader couldn't get through and "bite me with its fangs"!

After a while, I felt like I was sweating bullets, because I had been under the covers for so long. As I lay there breathing my own carbon dioxide, I remembered I was still clinging to my cell phone. How grateful I was for that! Usually it would have been plugged into the charger laying on my nightstand. I thanked God it was with me under the cover! Relieved, I remembered my phone had a built-in flashlight. After a few more minutes of waiting, I said to myself, "Pat, it's either you or the bat. You've got to figure out what you're going to do. Think!" So I began thinking, and decided I needed to find out more about this "invader" of my home and my domain.

Right then, I remembered the Bible saying something about 'knowing your enemy's devices', so I Googled "exterminators." (It was between 10 p.m. and 11 p.m., and most exterminators had already closed. So, the responses I got were recorded messages)! The more numbers I called, the more I thought I was NOT about to get anyone to come to my house in the middle of the night! One exterminator who actually answered even informed me it was against the law for me to kill a bat, because they are an endangered species! I was shocked! (If I had my way, he'd be worse than endangered)!

Disappointed, I began to "Google" 'bats' to find out facts about them I could use to my advantage. I discovered a bat *won't* attack unless cornered; I breathed a little sigh of relief, but not for long. Since my bedroom door was closed, I would need to summon my courage and figure a way for me to get out from under the covers, then cross the room to *open* my bedroom door, in hopes it would fly (or crawl) out. That was when the Holy Spirit challenged me firmly! Inside I heard, "Rise up and take authority over this bat AND THE FEAR that wants to dominate you! WORK the Word of God; you *know* it works!"

So, slowly (feeling a little embarrassed) I moved the covers just enough so one of my eyes could see out into the bedroom. After glancing in each corner of the room, I saw the bat; it was perched on the intake vent near the ceiling, RIGHT ABOVE MY BEDROOM DOOR! I was so disappointed! This meant I had to really encourage myself to be brave and go open the door.

Slowly, I eased myself completely from under the covers, moving quietly toward the door; then I s-l-o-w-l-y opened it. The bat didn't move. Cautiously, I left my room to check on other family members. When I returned, the bat had left the intake vent where I'd last seen it. I began to open other doors, remembering I had read that a bat will look for a way to escape from the house, if it can find one. I also learned a bat can't live longer than twenty-four hours without food. (Frankly, I hoped it would find its way out of my house OR DIE FROM STARVATION)! I thought, "Either solution will work for me." After all the drama, I was exhausted, so I rebuked the spirit of fear and fell asleep! I never encountered the bat again, but I learned a lot about my faith!

Now I think I know why God encourages believers to count it all joy when these kinds of experiences "try", "test", or "prove" the strength of our faith. If we never went through tests, our faith would be flabby-faith, which doesn't have the strength to help us accomplish the greater works Jesus said we would. I know, for sure, I had to change my mind *and my will*, before I could change my thinking, to find an effective strategy to execute. These changes had to happen *before* I could position my attitude to win in a situation where I had NO knowledge and NO desire to confront what was before me!

Apparently, *acting* on my faith caused a fearful situation to change, when *I decided* to change my *focus*. I'm so thankful to God His Word is profitable in every situation!

CHAPTER TEN

Choosing To Serve Under Authority

A Shepherding Pastor

Now, here is where I need to admit that early in my life, I had some proud, preconceived, even weird notions about people, and about my idea of what *I thought* I knew. I thought I knew what kind of preacher "I preferred" or from whom "*I thought*" I could best receive the preached Word. Back then, my attitude was like that of Naaman in the Bible, who was a Commander of the armies of Ben Hadad II, the king of Aram-Damascus. He was a good commander and was held in favor and high regard because of victories God brought him. Yet Naaman was a leper. (See II Kings, Chapter 5). In Scripture, leprosy speaks, figuratively, of a need for cleansing.

Unknown to me, I had apparently embraced propaganda (when I was younger) that people with a Southern accent or people from "down South" were unintelligent and unsophisticated. (Don't gasp! I asked God to forgive me for thinking like that, and He did). Now mind you, my siblings and I were all born in Virginia and so was our father. Our mother was born in North Carolina and later moved to Virginia, where she met our father. So, where did such deceiving notions come from? I don't know. Maybe they came, in part, from a spirit of pride, which could have been lurking deep within me, poisoning my mindset with skewed impressions of life and people from the time I was born. Or maybe, they came from a familiar spirit, which could have been in our family for generations! Who knows? (This is why I began to guard my children, grandchildren, and great grandchildren with heartfelt prayer concerning their thoughts, words and associations. *Prayer* is how we fight against spiritual influences because our fight is NOT against other people, whom God loved and paid a very dear price to redeem from soul destruction. We war *in prayer and wise loving actions* against any lie or prideful thought attempting to single anyone out as being "above" and therefore "better than everyone else.")

Still, God made us all and He knows everything about each of us. He knows our challenges, where we need to grow, and the best for each of His children. (I didn't know, then, but I was about to discover God also has a wise sense of humor)! I won't get into the details here, but God led me, supernaturally, to a fellowship of believers where He foreordained me to serve, and to the pastor He had handpicked—just for my spiritual maturity!

On my first visit to the church where He led me, a neatly dressed sixty-something Caucasian woman greeted me at the church's front door and asked, "Are you here for the satellite broadcast?" Although alone in the building, she was warm and friendly, inviting me to sit inside while we waited for others to arrive. (Incidentally, the guest satellite speaker was the same TV preacher whose teachings had fed me every Sunday for several months. Truth be told, I had really thought he was to speak in person, and if so, I wanted to get a good parking space; that's why I arrived so early). Then I noticed the large satellite dish in front of the building, and I "connected the dots". One other thing grabbed my attention: The woman who met me at the front door of the church said to me, "You're the person I talked to on the phone earlier, aren't you?" I said, "Yes" and quickly thought, "Wow, she remembered my voice!" That's when she introduced herself as "the pastor" of the church!

Turns out, she was born in South Carolina, and wouldn't you know it, she had an unmistakable Southern accent! (I told you God has a *wise sense of humor*)! Now I realized He was inducting me into the "Humility Curriculum" in His "School of the Holy Ghost".

Teacher

Through the faithfulness of this precious pastor, I learned so much about many things (and people). I grew in much needed spiritual and practical wisdom. I learned priceless lessons as I watched her live the Word of Truth she preached and taught. I also recall much of what I learned was "caught" rather than "taught". Everywhere she travelled, her way of living activated a culture of genuine support (for and from) many kinds of people and people groups.

Although it's impossible to mention all the ways she influenced me (and others), I learned essential disciplines from this committed under-shepherd who lived to give! I learned to *seek God* for my messages, whenever I taught. I remember the Sunday she pulled me aside and said, "Pat, the Lord wants you to know you can prophesy." I learned how to respect spiritual, civil and domestic authority, and how to receive strong, godly counsel. I accepted my license to minister the Gospel there and I learned to consult God's Spirit of Truth in prayer (and non-prayer) times. I learned the hard way how to keep God first in my relationships and follow His Biblical standards for handling the money, the family and the time he gave me to manage; I am still learning to do that part better.

Through this godly pastor's example of strong and relentless faith, I learned to apologize when I was wrong. I also learned how to remain firm in my faith during times of pain, adversity, embarrassment and change, while trusting God's faithful promises. I learned God's Word *always* reinforces the covenant rights Jesus died and rose again to secure for me, because I'm one of His children. Most importantly, I'm still learning who I am in Christ Jesus, because my old nature was crucified with Him! Since my old desires are dead (and still dying), I can recognize and catch their sly suggestions more easily, when they try to trick me into going backward to previous sins. I learned how my connection to God the Father, His Son and His Holy Spirit helps to shape my new spiritual character. I learned much from hearing her say, often, "People need love with skin on it", or "A hurried spirit is not of God", and of course "No one man or woman knows it all". I remember her wisely saying, "Don't throw out the baby with the bath water" and "Just eat the hay and leave the sticks", which I finally discovered is the meaning of I Thessalonians 5:21. (This was her advice whenever I read something I couldn't understand, or listened to someone preach a message I couldn't receive right away). These are just some of the nuggets of truth I keep in my little "bag of smooth stones" like David used when he challenged and defeated Goliath! She had many more nuggets of wisdom, such as whenever I left a counseling session with her she'd say, "We won't discuss this again because you've repented and it's now under the Blood of Jesus. Let's leave it there."

Watching her example, I learned to dress myself in fashionable clothes complimenting my own unique body type without compromising God's standards of decency and self-control. Perhaps most importantly, I learned to forgive quickly those who hurt me, stole from me, lied about me, set me up; and even those who may find it difficult to forgive me for wrongs I perpetrated against them; or maybe when I committed no wrong, but they had convinced themselves I had. She showed me that forgiveness and unconditional love always work; and, oh yes, "Money answers all things" (Ecclesiastes 10:19).

Pastor Jackie Norris counseled me while I overcame overt and secret sins. She loved me while I "sat on the pew for a while" until I recharged my spirit to regain a godly and accurate perspective of God's wisdom and ways. She prayed for me and encouraged me to be a strong, godly leader as I continued my journey to Christ-likeness under the Holy Spirit's faithful watch.

For more than twenty-five years, I observed how God worked supernatural gifts through her, Words of knowledge—revealing hidden things; interpretation of tongues; supernatural healings, dreams, visions and more whenever the Holy Spirit wanted to use her obedience. I watched her model pastoral love by genuinely accepting everyone of every personality, ethnicity, and socio-economic category. She interceded for all of us, assuring us of the Holy Spirit's faithfulness to teach us, uniquely, as He completes the good things Christ began in each of us when we first believed and trusted His power to change us! I'd like to say much more, but space cannot accommodate the full unfolding of a life such as hers, so well lived!

When, willingly and peacefully, she went to be in God's nearer presence—full of years and full of wisdom, she left a legacy I want to continue following until I finish my journey on earth. As I decided to serve under the protection of God-ordained authority, God has been faithful to come and reveal each step on my path to His New, and better, Covenant!

The Takeaway: "And I will give you shepherds after my own heart, who will guide you with knowledge and understanding." (Jeremiah 3:15 NLT)

CHAPTER ELEVEN

Choosing To Stay With The Process

"I pondered the direction of my life, and I turned to follow your laws." (Psalm 119:59 NLT)

I could have made excuses and run many times. I could have quit my assignment when I was bored, disillusioned, wounded, or scared, but God helped me choose *His* will, and I did not leave my assigned place. I chose to stay because *my Lord* had assigned me to my place of service. Our founding Pastor frequently said, "Pat, if they just wouldn't run off...." What she meant was, if the "sheep" would decide (choose) to engage the challenges of day-to-day mistakes, misunderstandings and relational conflicts, they could actually change for the better until the Holy Spirit reassigned them to a different place of service (in His *due* season).

"It's not so much the stories we can tell, but our decisions and how we grow from them."

God's Commitment to Help Me Change

My willingness to experience life from a divine perspective is realigning my affections-the things *I* like. Gradually, God's desires are becoming my desires and He helps me choose to move, optimizing the spiritual gifts He deposited in me for *His* use. He does it for the good of all. As I ask for His mercy, He forgives all my new mistakes, because of His vast love. In His wisdom, He continues to help me dodge "stumbling blocks", as I learn to follow Him closely.

He's doing the same for you, in case you haven't noticed. Daily, He loads us with new mercies and fresh opportunities to evaluate if our own plans and choices are productive. By His grace, He wants us to find better ways of choosing (and doing) right. He'll show us fresh ways to love others, willingly and unselfishly. (I must confess, unconditional love requires "true grit" to stretch the mind and mature the soul)!

I have also noticed my level of willingness is directly proportionate to the level of success I actually achieve. As I continually embrace an "attitude of willingness", psychological barriers fall, making it easier for me to take the next step toward living out my destiny, as pre-written about me in God's Book of life!

Dancing Lady

Oddly, I've seen a middle-aged woman dancing barefoot around my community, and she moves her body, as if to music, but her mind appears to be somewhere else. At first, I thought she was exercising to music on her smart phone, but looking closer, her focus appeared to be somewhere else. She never changes her routine and her scanty clothes don't appear to be appropriate for the weather, regardless of the season. My heart breaks for her.

The first time I saw her, I caught myself desperately whispering a quick prayer to God, "Oh God, what...how...do you want me to help this lady?" I thought He might want me to approach her with kind words of help or compassion, to try to help her. Then I heard His Holy Spirit urge me, "Pray for her." So whenever I see her, I pray.

Seeing her reminded me of a time when my own peace of mind was so assaulted, I felt trapped and terrified. I didn't know I was in deep depression.

Later, I would learn God had provided a "garment" of praise to lift me above depression's smothering weight. Until then, I found out the hard way depression is a dark, suffocating spirit, seeking to destroy its victim.

Back then, I usually ran *from* "fight-or-flight" situations. Now fear had driven me into depression so deep that anxiety ruled my days! We had relocated to a Southern military installation, away from relatives and friends, and only communicated with extended family by phone or an occasional letter. I ran up some hefty long-distance telephone bills during our ten months there. (Back then, there was no free, unlimited long-distance calling).

I was running high on self-pity and low on coping strategies, as I tried to handle the complicated madness of young family life in a fallen world. After rejecting "happy hour" at the NCO Club on post and watching TV soap operas for relief, I was desperate to find peace. Two or three months into searching for "normalcy", I resorted to prayer. I thought, "Maybe prayer can help me sort out how to adapt to this new life I don't seem to fit into or want." The relocation was challenging me to change in ways I never expected!

Whenever I prayed, my prayers seemed to go no further than the room where I was, so I started phoning family back home for advice and encouragement. (We had not yet found a church to go to, which added to my feelings of alienation and isolation). I constantly wished we were back in Maryland, but I knew I had to tackle this new experience. So, I willed my mind to stay and "fight to feel normal". There was only one problem with my choice—I'd never learned to fight well. (I would quickly learn, though, now that I was "in the trenches"). I was in a low emotional place and my thoughts were full of terrifying "what if's".

I didn't know about spiritual warfare back then, so I felt powerless against the negative thoughts blindsiding me. All I knew about was "religion". I was moping and crying, worrying about everything! I felt trapped and out-gunned, and I know the devil was probably jumping for joy right about then! I'm sure he thought he had cornered me for sure!

One day, I heard one of our neighbors had suffered a fatal brain aneurism. Fear gripped me so tightly it convinced me the same thing would soon "take me out"! I was afraid even to sleep or eat. I'd prepare breakfast, then call the children to join me, as I blessed the food. Then, all of a sudden, I just couldn't eat it. As soon as I'd raise my fork to eat, a "lump of anxiety" would rise into my chest and throat, threatening to cut off my breath! I was starving, but I just couldn't bring myself to put food in my mouth! Things got so bad, I lost one pound a day for six consecutive days! Soon it got so bad I couldn't stay in a room by myself. Fear and anxiety so overwhelmed me, I'd call the children to play with their toys in the same room where I was. This eased the fear a little, and chased away its threat to overwhelm me. The precious innocence of my two toddlers seemed to be the only neutralizer for such mounting anxiety. I'm so glad they were completely oblivious to how I was really feeling. Their innocent love refreshed me and brought me temporary peace.

When I finally visited a doctor, he patiently listened to my story and my symptoms. Once he heard what I'd been going through, he diagnosed my condition as "Severe Depression". He then prescribed some little blue pills, the name of which I've forgotten, but they only relieved the depression for few days. So, I had to take more just to get the "artificial peace" I felt with the first dose. A week later, the depression had not diminished; it lasted for months until we went home for a Christmastime visit.

During our visit, we stayed with my oldest sister's family, where we had fun eating, playing board games and talking as we had done in the past. Once, during a short break from one of our board games, I excused myself to take my medicine and she became curious about the pills I was taking. Asking to see the container, she read the label on the bottle, then promptly dumped all the pills down the toilet, and that was the end of that. Resolutely, she turned and said to me, "If you start feeling anxious again, just take two aspirin." I knew she was no doctor, but my oldest sister's advice was like "gold" to me. Clearly, she was the anchor I needed at that critical time. The anxiety attacks stopped after that.

Back in our military home, I tried to pray whenever I felt anxious. I still felt like I was groping in overwhelming fog, searching for stability from the God I knew with my parents, but I couldn't seem to find Him. (I didn't realize God's Holy Spirit was always with me, because I had never really worked at building much of a spiritual love-relationship with Him. I guess that's why it was hard to discern His voice from all the other distractions).

By God's grace, I slowly began noticing how the Holy Spirit was quietly teaching me to dispel fear with joy, and reading my Bible began to excite me. I noticed how sadness changed to relief when I'd take time out to thank God for ordinary things. Depression really dissolved whenever I praised God *loudly*! My spirit lifted as snippets of melodies and lyrics to old hymns brought new hope! Soon, songs of rejoicing became my songs of deliverance! To this day, joyful praise and thanks remain my greatest allies to escape rollercoaster emotions and stressful situations.

Months passed before I gained enough wisdom (and courage) to move back home permanently, but God helped me. He was my "Change Agent", sending people to help when I needed it most. Back home, I made a conscious choice to fight off self-pity. Instead, I chose to let spiritual songs and hymns "sing themselves" in the background of my mind until they filled my heart and my mouth to overflowing.

I've learned our choices for dealing with pressing issues can take us way up *or* way down. Life is hard because we don't always choose right, and the devil is busy taking advantage of every one of our bad choices. He harasses anyone who wanders from the sheltered place of God's word—NO EXCEPTIONS! He means to deceive us, so he can steal our God-given authority through seduction and trickery, hoping to take us out of the end-time game.

Now I realize I must choose to go "up" in prayer and praise, whenever I feel a downward pull to do or say something negative. I must press to ascend to the sphere of "higher praise" until it liberates me! We have "weapons of spiritual warfare" (see Ephesians, Chapter 6) to frustrate, delay and stop attacks waged against us by the evil one. They are God's promises in our mouths, spoken with purpose! Evil influences are *allergic* to praise! Praising whenever we can, makes (and keeps) us free from depression and fear. I've learned as I pray, God the Holy Spirit prays *through* me, so I can use my God-given authority from Jesus Christ to decree truth and agree with what *God says* is true.

*God never wants us to feel down and displaced. Feeling bad or defeated is *our* choice and it will keep us down as long as we permit it. The joy of the Lord will keep pushing upward through depression until we embrace its upward push! Like the "dancing lady", we can choose our own ways of coping with life's blunt force traumas *or* we can choose to put on a garment of praise to throw off the spirit of depression and rejoice over God's faithfulness! Now *I* have become "*a rejoicing lady*"! It's not always easy, but dancing and rejoicing with uplifted hands invites God to "cut in and dance with me!" In the Bible He says He delights in "twirling around" and acting "clamorously foolish" as we dance together! If it sounds silly, that's the point. The more I delight myself in His presence and provision, the more my spirit soars!

If you'll surrender by calling out to God, He will bend the heavens and move mountains to swoop down and lift *you* back up to where you belong, to your position of active authority!

Wisdom Word: Just ASK the Savior to help you; He will carry you through.

CHAPTER TWELVE

Choosing To Turn Around

"Without a change in course, there can be no change in destination." *Rabbi Jonathan Cahn*

God's "unchangeable" nature stands as a witness that everything and everyone else in *His* created world (and universe) *must* change, as they revolve around His changeless will.

In his Divine wisdom, God grants everyone new beginnings in time and opportunity, *and* He has established order in the earth through "cycles".

The Bible teaches me that *every* human being senses a timeline on his or her longevity. God "has also planted eternity [a sense of divine purpose] in the human heart [a mysterious longing which nothing under the sun can satisfy, except God]—yet man cannot find out (comprehend, grasp) what God has done (His overall plan) from the beginning to the end..... "He has made everything beautiful and appropriate in its time." (Ecclesiastes. 3:11 AMP) [Emphasis added].

God also said, *"As long as the earth remains, there will be planting and harvest, cold and heat, summer and winter, day and night." (Genesis 8:22 NLT)* Whenever God says something "will be", we can be sure it will happen just as He said it would.

His immutable laws work, in spite of our disbelief. However, He also has set some things "outside the scope" of our freedom of choice. They are under His purview and are therefore immutable (unchangeable), because the mouth of the Lord has said it will be a certain way. He will *not* alter the Word He has spoken. (See Psalm 89, Verse 34)

Let's consider, for a moment, this planet on which we live. God chose to tell us about the stable things of the earth that *never* change, although many things on the earth *do* change. Knowing and believing this, should motivate us to confidently persevere and expect His help as we complete our God-assignments. He is "All-Knowing" and we can trust His will for us. We can learn to trust Him by taking our first step of faith, which believes God exists. Based on that belief, we can then *act* on what we believe He has asked us to do. Afterward, He rewards our diligent search for Him, where we discover He actually is a *real* Person who keeps His Word.

On the other hand, God has chosen to show us many things *do* change in the earth, like seasons. Other things, which *should* change, are the hearts and attitudes of people, whom He put in control of their own will. Expecting imminent change, can help us move *forward* (away from fear of the future and past mistakes), as we anticipate good things to come.

Throughout time, many have echoed their observations regarding the human need for change. Others blame their woes on the powerful impact change has had on their emotions and choices. This book focuses more on how to use *our* will to *agree with* the *good will* of God, which is the avenue to lasting and effective change. Many poems capture observable truths about the undeniable handiwork of God's miraculous creation, in nature and people. They echo the message that eventually, every "thing" changes, either in physical form, maturity of heart, or both. Most observe that nothing stays the same.

The very nature of normal human growth is cyclical, sequential and/or seasonal. Intrinsically, we expect to change as we mature through different stages of development, according to our God-designed inner clock. Surely, young people grow old, whether we like it or not. No thing or person remains unchanged. Truth is: all created things will change. However, God, our Creator is *not* a created being nor is He a created thing. He is the First Cause of everything, and therefore, changeless!

We agree with God when we acknowledge His handiwork, such as rain coming from the clouds and sun lighting up the sky. When birds fly past us, we witness the will and might of Almighty God. Each year as winter submits to a new season of life, we observe new life and beauty, and we somehow know life always continues. Through the process of change, God reminds everyone our wounded hearts can also heal! Yes, for all who have suffered emotional wounds, those hearts can heal, *if we choose* to *ask God* to heal us. Our hearts can heal because God has wired our human minds and bodies to be whole and functional, (in the right environment). It is the environment of faith in His Name: Jehovah Rapha. God wants to keep healing us.

As a new mother forgets the hard-searing pains associated with the birthing process, we can choose to replace painful experiences the more we focus on the love and grace of God, which change every kind of painful experience. Hearing God's spoken promises, causes faith for healing to become real and tangible, as we remain saturated in the presence and promise of His healing Word.

As His children, we must continually remind ourselves God made us wonderfully complex! He made us resilient, as He is. Do not permit the adversary of all humanity to captivate you with lies and beguiling deceptions. He wants to seduce you into dwelling on warped thoughts. He wants to accuse you. He wants *you* to say you are weak or meaningless or, worse:

unimportant! We who belong to Christ are all children of the only God, the Most High—the Living God! In the book of I John, Chapter 3, the Love Apostle (John) writes to believers, reminding us of who we *really are* and of our mission *and* responsibility to change, so we can love as our Father God loves.

The human standard for loving is, at best, a moving target. If we allow our minds to be deceived, thinking *we* have "figured it all out"; if we try to remain suspended in a state of "comfort with the familiar" or if we try to love according to any standard other than God's, our efforts will always plummet and fizzle out. This kind of thinking plunges us into deep depression and feelings of hopelessness and helplessness, because it's connected to pride. When we become mentally stagnant and trapped by corrupt thoughts, we taint and even stall our progress. The "greater works" Jesus decreed we will do, and the greater glory, happen when we daily admit our need for God's present help. He alone has the greatest kind of love: Redeeming Love! He wants to help us stay focused on what's beautiful, rare and priceless!

He alone has the greatest plan for our lives, which saves to the uttermost! He planned for each of us to have *and manage* the greatest prosperity imaginable! It includes an eternity of joyous fellowship with all who have accepted relationship in God's family circle.

His circle of "family-fellowship" began the moment each of us confessed Jesus, the Messiah as our only Lord, and His circle of harmonious family-love will reach its fullness when the greatest harvest of souls for Heaven has been "forever changed" to be with God in real relationship throughout all eternity! The more we experience God's extravagant, protective (and corrective) love here on earth, the more His love works within us to change our hearts. "Repenting" (changing) involves *showing evidence we have changed.* Do not allow yourself to be deceived or distracted from this truth: ONLY GOD'S PLAN BRINGS UNITY AND REAL CHANGE. The person who *wants* to obey God will change to adjust their thinking, their decisions and their actions to align with His divine plan no matter how tough.

If you really believe you are the captain of your own ship, also remember every successful captain accepts *and submits* to orders from a higher chain of command. The successful captain obeys those orders for the good of everyone traveling on-board. Alone, one person might handle the operation of a small vessel, but handling a ship requires the cooperation of many people respectfully submitting to one other's authority because they all submit to the same orders from their highest command.

As we submit to what *God says* is right, we mature the aromatic fruit of spiritual wisdom and self-control, making us attractive to others. People usually seek to be with those who take time to be interested in them. *Are you willing to change your attitude toward the God of Heaven so you can be ready to extend God's love to other people?* He loves you with an abiding Fatherly love. He also gave you awesome potential for change. Your likeliness to change, however, depends on *you*. Only you can determine your momentum of change, as you decide to use your gift of free will the way God uniquely planned.

Reader: As you have read about God's dealings with me during my continuing process of maturity, He also gives you time and opportunity to *choose* change, (a 180-degree change).

Time, unfortunately, is winding down...Jesus *is* coming soon and with His return, the Age of Grace *will* end. You can speed up your maturity now by making Jesus your *Lord* (not just your Savior), and seizing opportunities to spread the Good News of His return through the wholesome life *you* live.

Micah 6:8 reminds us, *"But he's already made it plain how to live, what to do, what God is looking for in men and women. It's quite simple: Do what is fair and just to your neighbor, be compassionate and loyal in your love, and don't take yourself too seriously-Take God seriously."*

The Message